EDUCATION
ON
THE DALTON PLAN

Introduction

   The impulse to record our past and to derive some sense of meaning from it is part of the human need to know who we are ... The Dalton School is a significant part of the lives of those who are its students and its faculty ... It is also the bearer of its own values, ideals and traditions; to understand why it was founded and how it evolved is to gain valuable insight into the history of American education.

Diane Ravitch
Adjunct Associate Professor
of History and Education
Teachers College,
Columbia University

   During the Sixtieth Anniversary celebration of The Dalton School in the 1980-81 year, many Dalton parents, faculty and alumni inquired about *Education on the Dalton Plan* by Helen Parkhurst. This is the book in which Miss Parkhurst describes the history and implementation of the Dalton Plan, and the beginnings of The Dalton School. Unfortunately, the book was out of print at the time of our anniversary festivities, and we could only refer people to the few copies available in the Dalton library.

   Given the considerable interest in *Education on The Dalton Plan,* we have published this special reprinting to commemorate the Sixtieth Anniversary of the School.

Dr. Gardner P. Dunnan
Headmaster
The Dalton School
New York City

January, 1982

In 1922, Helen Parkhurst published *Education on The Dalton Plan,* a volume that was quickly translated into fourteen languages. In many ways, that book is as important to the world of education today as it was then.

At that time, Ms. Parkhurst was listed as "Education Director of The Children's University School," a small but vibrant school located on the West Side that was, two years later, to be renamed The Dalton School.

When Dalton celebrated its 60th anniversary, we reprinted Parkhurst's book in response to many requests. It has been widely distributed and is given regularly to every newly hired teacher at Dalton.

This year, as we celebrate the 75th anniversary of The Dalton School, it is fitting that *Education on The Dalton Plan* be reprinted again, for it contains the essence of Helen Parkhurst's remarkable vision—a vision that continues to guide our work.

Dr. Gardner P. Dunnan
Headmaster
The Dalton School
New York City

September, 1994

A 75th anniversary is always a special occasion. At Dalton, this celebration affords us the opportunity to both reflect on our vibrant history and look forward to a bright and exciting future.

The unique qualities that have made Dalton so extraordinary were first articulated by Helen Parkhurst in her book *Education on The Dalton Plan.*

We are pleased that it has been reprinted as part of Dalton's 75th anniversary celebration.

Norma Smith and Randy Smith Aberg '78
Co-Chairpersons
75th Anniversary Committee

September, 1994

EDUCATION

ON

THE DALTON PLAN

BY

HELEN PARKHURST

EDUCATION DIRECTOR, CHILDREN'S UNIVERSITY SCHOOL

With an Introduction by

T. P. NUNN, M.A., D.Sc.

PROFESSOR OF EDUCATION, UNIVERSITY OF LONDON AND
HEAD OF LONDON DAY TRAINING COLLEGE,
UNIVERSITY OF LONDON

Contributions by

ROSA BASSETT, M.B.E., B.A.

AND JOHN EADES

NEW YORK

E. P. DUTTON & COMPANY

681 FIFTH AVENUE

"There is a sort of mysterious upheaval of mankind in the way
new things spring up, which commands our awe. At a given hour,
anything wanted by the race makes its appearance simultaneously
from so many quarters, that the title of a single individual to
discovery is always contested and seems clearly to belong to God
manifested through man."

EDWARD SEGUIN.

FOREWORD

I wish to take this opportunity of expressing my gratitude for the unfailing sympathy and support accorded to me and my work by the Parents' Committee, and the Faculty of the Children's University School; by Ernest Jackman, Principal of the Dalton High School; to Dr. M. V. O'Shea of Wisconsin University; to Miss Helen Hutchins Weist, who has assisted me in England and America; and to Mr. John Macrae, Vice President of E. P. Dutton & Co., whose interest and foresight brought out Miss Evelyn Dewey's book on the Dalton Laboratory Plan, giving to the educational public the first literature on the Dalton Plan.

Among those to whom I am indebted in England for advice and encouragement are Sir Michael Sadler, Mr. Edmond Holmes, Dr. C. W. Kimmins, and Professor T. P. Nunn, who has kindly contributed the introduction to this book. My thanks are also due to Miss Rosa Bassett who was the first to introduce the plan in the largest girls' secondary school in London, and to Mr. John Eades, head master of a large boys' school in Leeds, who have contributed valuable accounts of experiments with the Dalton Laboratory Plan.

HELEN PARKHURST.

Children's University School.
  June, 1922.

CONTENTS

PAGE

INTRODUCTION. By T. P. NUNN, M.A., D.Sc.,
Professor, Department of Education, University of London and Head of London
Day Training College, University of
London   xi

CHAPTER

I. THE INCEPTION OF THE DALTON LABORATORY PLAN   1

II. THE PLAN IN PRINCIPLE   18

III. THE PLAN IN PRACTICE   34

IV. ITS APPLICATION—A CONCRETE EXAMPLE   .   45

V. ASSIGNMENTS—HOW TO MAKE THEM   . .   57

VI. SAMPLE ASSIGNMENTS   72

VII. THE GRAPH METHOD OF RECORDING
PROGRESS   134

VIII. TEACHING AND LEARNING   150

IX. A YEAR'S EXPERIMENT IN AN ENGLISH
SECONDARY SCHOOL. By ROSA BASSETT,
M.B.E., M.A., Head Mistress, The County
Secondary School for Girls, Streatham   .   175

CHAPTER   PAGE

X. THE DALTON PLAN FOR ELEMENTARY
   SCHOOLS. By JOHN EADES, Head Master,
   Kirkstall Road School, Leeds . . . 196

APPENDIX

I. ASSIGNMENTS WHICH HAVE BEEN USED IN
   BRITISH ELEMENTARY SCHOOLS . . . 227

II. ASSIGNMENTS WHICH HAVE BEEN USED IN THE
    COUNTY SECONDARY SCHOOL, STREATHAM 249

III. SOME OPINIONS OF BRITISH ELEMENTARY
     HEAD MISTRESSES AND CHILDREN ON
     THE DALTON PLAN 269

INTRODUCTION

TEACHING and learning are correlative occupations which have been carried on since the beginnings of human society. In this book Miss Helen Parkhurst inquires how they may best be adjusted to one another, and offers a definite answer to the question.

To many persons, teachers as well as laymen, both inquiry and answer may seem, at this time of day, to be superfluous. Does not everyone know well enough what it is to be taught and to learn? And is not discussion of so simple a matter bound to prove one of those exercises in word-spinning which delight pedants and cranks, but are a cause of just irritation to sensible people? To these objections it is enough to reply that the matter cannot be so simple, for it is one upon which wide and important differences of opinion have existed, and still exist. A fresh debate, conducted in the practical spirit which inspires the following pages, must therefore be useful, if it does no more than challenge us to re-examine accepted ideas and reassure ourselves of their soundness. In education, as in all the arts of life, a certain "scepticism of the instrument" (as Mr. Wells has called it) is constantly needed if progress is not to end in the stagnation of routine.

The central question about teaching and learning may be put thus: What is the proper distribution of initiative and responsibility between teacher and taught? The answer to be given obviously depends upon the pupil's natural attitude towards learning, his insight (conscious or unconscious) into his own needs, and the strength of his will to satisfy them. Upon these points very pessimistic views once prevailed. A boy, it was held, cannot possibly know what is good for him, and having crept, like a snail, unwillingly to school, will learn there only what he is made to learn. Initiative and responsibility belong, then, almost wholly to his teachers. It is for them to decide not only what shall be taught, but also how and when it shall be learnt; the boy's share in the business is simply to perform his task—or, failing that, to pay the penalty attached to laziness, stupidity, or contumacy. This theory does not actually deny that boys and girls have natural interests and are keen to pursue them, but it regards them as the foe, rather than the friend, of the schoolmaster. "Go and see what Budge and Tod are doing, and tell them not to" expresses its general attitude towards the initiative of youth. As regards school learning, its working hypothesis is the idea that the child's mind is a wax tablet scraped clean to receive such characters as the teacher may choose to impress on it, or (as

Dickens' Mr. M'Choakumchild thought) an empty vessel to be filled at his discretion with "imperial gallons of fact."

In its cruder forms this view will hardly be found now in any responsible quarter. Even Mr. Bernard Shaw, who thinks so poorly of schools, does not deny that boys and girls are often far happier in them than outside. And there is no doubt that they are happier and spend their schooldays more profitably than they used to do because the modern schoolmaster has, so to speak, recognized their natural activities officially, and allows them to be to some extent partners in the management of their own lives—in short, because Mr. M'Choakumchild is definitely dead. Nevertheless, it is possible for a cynic to maintain that his soul goes marching on and will continue to do so while two institutions stand which, taken together, express the essence of his educational philosophy. Those institutions are the customary school time-table and the customary system of class instruction. For the time-table originated in the assumption that the teacher should dictate what his pupils are to do at every hour of their school lives, and the class-system in the belief that he may ignore the varied modes and rates of movement which distinguish one mind from another, and may treat five and twenty minds (or a hundred) as if they were one.

Now it may be said in defence that an institution may be very valuable, even though its origin be disreputable; that "whate'er is best administered is best"; and that, as a matter of fact, an immense amount of good work is done in schools where no alternative to the class method has ever been thought of. These things are doubtless true. The old machinery has been captured by a new spirit; but the very competence and humanity with which it is now handled have led many observers to "scepticism of the instrument"—have led them, that is, to doubt whether the class-method has not pressed far beyond its limits of usefulness, and whether it should not be supplemented, if not wholly replaced, by another.

Some time ago the writer of these lines expressed such doubts in a passage which—since it looks beyond the disease to a possible remedy—he may be allowed to quote:

*"You all know how a familiar word, persistently stared at suddenly becomes almost alarmingly strange and meaningless—how (as William James said) it seems to glare back from the page with no speculation in its eyes. You will have something like the same uncanny experience if you watch the operation of a school time-table after rigorously clearing your mind of its familiar associations. From 10.15 to 11.00 twenty-five souls are simultaneously engrossed in the theory

* From a Presidential Address to the Mathematical Association. Printed in the *Mathematical Gazette* for March, 1918.

of quadratic equations; at the very stroke of the hour their interest in this subject suddenly expires, and they all demand exercise in French phonetics! Like the agreement of actors on the stage, 'their unanimity is wonderful'—but also, when one comes to think of it, ludicrously artificial. Can we devise no way of conducting our business that would bring it into better accord with the natural ebb and flow of interest and activity? It may be that the specialist system, often a tireless complication of the present arrangements, would make a fluid organization perfectly feasible. There must still be, no doubt, certain fixed periods for collective work; but during the rest of the day each specialist's room might be a 'pupil room' in which boys or girls of all standing would work, singly or in groups, in independence of one another, and for variable lengths of time. It would, of course, be necessary to record each pupil's progress and to see that he followed a reasonable programme of studies, but I find no reason why in such matters methods like those of the Caldecott Community should not be universalized."

Years before these words were uttered the speaker, like numberless other teachers, had worked something like this plan with a group of senior pupils; and he had before his mind, of

course, Professor Dewey's work and Miss
Mason's, and especially the striking reforms in
the education of young children inspired by Dr.
Montessori. But he was quite unaware that what
he put forward as a dream of the future was, while
he spoke, an actual fact on the farther side of the
Atlantic. It was left to Miss Belle Rennie to add
to her many services to progress in education by
bringing Miss Parkhurst's courageous and well-
thought-out experiment to the notice of British
teachers.

Miss Rennie's brief account of the "Dalton
Laboratory Plan" appeared in the Education Supplement of *The Times* in May, 1920, and her
swollen post-bag began at once to show how widely
dissatisfaction with the class-method is spread and
how many teachers are looking for a better instrument of instruction. One month later, a large-
scale repetition of the American experiment was
initiated by Miss Rosa Bassett at the Streatham
County Secondary School; in August the first vin-
tage of her results were discussed at the Cardiff
meeting of the British Association. Thereafter,
interest grew so rapidly that, in July, 1921, when
Miss Parkhurst came to England, accommodation
could not be found for all who wished to hear her
expound the "plan," and when Miss Bassett
opened the doors of her school to inquirers for
three days the roads of Streatham were encum-
bered with over two thousand pilgrims!

Nothing need be said here about the plan itself,

for Miss Parkhurst explains it with careful detail in the following chapters, and Miss Bassett has added an account of her experience in adapting it to the conditions of a large English secondary school. It is, however, permissible to one who has the honour of introducing the book to its public, to commend the scientific temper in which it is written. Miss Parkhurst has envisaged a definite problem of great practical importance: namely, how to secure from the vast volume of educational effort expended in schools a richer harvest of individual culture and efficiency. The "Dalton Laboratory Plan" is her solution. No one recognizes more clearly than she that there are others, and that her own is not final, but is susceptible of useful modification and development. When Dr. Montessori's work became known in this country, the movement towards what is somewhat barbarously called "auto-education" received a remarkable impulse. Everywhere reformers are now busy opening up and exploring new ways of conducting the ancient work of education. Some are "wilder comrades," sworn to cut themselves off from the old tradition and everything that belongs to it. These may regard as a miserable compromise a scheme which does not demand even the abolition of public examinations! But to no less adventurous spirits, who would hasten slowly and keep on firm ground, the "Dalton Plan" offers a path of progress which may safely be taken by all who have the gifts of intelligence, devotion, and enterprise.

Boldness and originality are typical qualities of American education, and we may hope that the present close and happy association between an American teacher and the English men and women who are following her lead may also become typical. Typically American, too, is the generosity which has prompted Miss Parkhurst to assign her pecuniary interest in this book to a noble English institution—the Heritage Craft School for Crippled Children at Chailey. On all grounds we may wish good-speed to her enterprise.

T. P. NUNN.

UNIVERSITY OF LONDON,
April, 1922.

EDUCATION
ON
THE DALTON PLAN

EDUCATION ON THE DALTON PLAN

CHAPTER I

The Inception of the Dalton Laboratory Plan

Among American thinkers Emerson was one of the first to realize and to point out that our educational system was a failure because the ideals upon which it had been founded had lost their meaning. "We are students of words," he wrote, "we are shut up in schools and colleges and recitation rooms for ten or fifteen years and come out at last with a bag of wind, a memory of words, and do not know a thing." In a recent interview Thomas Edison, whose only formal education consisted of "some instruction from his mother" echoed this indictment. "The possibilities for the development of the human brain are," he said, "almost infinite. But the important thing is not to make young children study the thing they don't like, for the moment school is not as interesting as play it is an injury. I don't know exactly at what age a child's mind atrophies, but it is somewhere between eleven and fourteen. If you make a child study things he doesn't care for, and keep this up until he is fourteen, his brain will be impaired forever. Children naturally like to learn. They possess great curiosity but they must be interested in the subject. Our educational methods fail to do this. Change these methods, and many more 'freaks' will be produced. I am a 'freak' myself."

Is it any wonder therefore that in the United States, where every man can be educated at the expense of his state, the percentage of failures in colleges and universities is said to be greater to-day than at any previous time in our history. Formerly when the educational field was much narrower than it is now only a selected few went to college. They were the mental superiors in each family, chosen for their supposed fitness to enjoy the benefits of higher education. Thus they were judged and labelled as superior specimens even before they were submitted to the educational process. As a result they returned from college more or less as they went into it. Education was at that time considered a privilege and the educated became automatically a class apart, exempt from criticism. Their crystallized attitude, which school had only served to confirm, cut them off from the simpler men and women whose offspring they were. How could they have anything in common with the parental struggle and sacrifice which had made it possible for them to enjoy these advantages? They were, if anything, less able to share the common lot, having bartered their simplicity for a pedestal of intellectual passivity which rendered them useless to society at home or at large.

That was the United States of yesterday. To-day the very meaning of education has changed. It is no longer regarded as an end in itself and for every single individual who set out in search of it in the past there are now fifty. So universal is the demand for education that the minority which remains indifferent to its advantages has become negligible. With schools and colleges filled to overflowing educationalists are face to face with new problems, both spiritual and material. The demand is not only infinitely greater than ever before, but it is also a different kind of demand. In the old days the student went to school to get what the school had to offer him; now he goes to school to satisfy a definite need for self-development. He is no longer disposed to learn just what the teacher proposes to teach. The mould that has done for past generations of pupils will no longer do for him.

Unfortunately the men and women who work by the old system and live by it are not only naturally interested in its preservation but they almost in-inevitably lose the power to judge of it impersonally. Their minds become encrusted like the system itself. And though there are many sincere and well-disposed persons among them they are apt to become, through devoting all their energies to the task of "keeping up the old traditions," incapable of re-kindling the torch of truth. Such people continue to regard themselves as the consecrated leaders of youth—leaders whose authority cannot be disputed. They continue to judge the new and varied crowd of students by the same old standards. Nothing will induce them to scrap the outworn routine for a fresh and vital method made to fit a fresh and vital humanity.

More criticism of the educational system comes from the parents of pupils. On every side one hears the question asked, "What has my daughter got out of her college training?" and again, "How has the university fitted my son for the battle of life?" The answer of the schools that they provide "experience" is only valid after a definition of what experience really is. The pioneers of the early days of American history were usually men who were quite uneducated in the academic sense of the word. Experience was their only school. Their inborn talents alone enabled them to learn the supreme lesson of life. They were the survivors who fought and conquered. But what of those who fell in the battle and who might with the aid of some educational experience have given a good account of themselves? To-day we cannot afford so high a proportion of derelicts. We have got to find some way of expanding and strengthening the natural talents of the average boy before he goes forth into the wide struggle for life and success. We have got to provide opportunities for the average girl to learn not only how to develop her intellect but also how to conduct herself as a unit of society.

In order to acquire these two kinds of experience while we are still immature beings a favourable environment is the first essential. On this point Edwin G. Conklin writes in an illuminating way in his book *Heredity and Environment*. According to this author "Only that environment and training are good which lead to the development of good habits and traits or to the suppression of bad ones. . . . In general the best environment is one which avoids extremes, one which is neither too easy nor too hard, one which produces maximum efficiency of mind and body."

"In education we are strangely blind to proper aims and methods. Any education is bad which leads to the formation of habits of idleness, carelessness, failure, instead of industry, thoroughness and success. Any religion or social institution is bad which leads to habits of pious makebelieve, insincerity, slavish regard for authority and disregard for evidence, instead of habits of sincerity, open-mindedness and independence."

These are the beacon lights towards which education should tend. By its works on the pupils we shall know it. Has our educational system succeeded in making the children upon whom it has been imposed industrious, sincere, open-minded and independent? The answer must certainly be in the negative. This is not, however, to say that those qualities can only be developed at the sacrifice of the old and purely cultural values to the attainment of which the efforts of educationalists have been hitherto exclusively devoted. It is possible to inculcate a respect for learning and the desire for a high level of cultural development and at the same time to breed in the young that moral stamina upon which Edwin Conklin sets such price and which is indispensable to good and abundant living. But this twin ideal will only be reached if school life is modified as so to include training in real experience—that experience for which a craving exists in every youthful heart. The child must be fortified to solve the problems of childhood before he comes face to face with the problem of youth and maturity. He can only do this if education is designed to give him such freedom and responsibility as will permit him to tackle them for and by himself. Experience is that and nothing more. Without it no development of character is possible, and without character no problems can be satisfactorily solved at any age. The child, cramped and frustrated by the rules and regulations of our educational system, never gets to grips with experience in any form. He neither learns to master his own difficulties nor the difficulties bred of contact with his fellows.

It is indeed almost impossible to over-estimate the value of such experience to the child as to the adult. It tests as nothing else can test the moral and intellectual fibre of the individual. It shapes and tempers his thoughts, sharpens and enlarges his judgment, teaching at the same time the most important lesson of all—self-discipline—as the individual comes into relation with other individuals. Group consciousness grows out of this social experience. Only by bringing it into the daily lives of our children can we give back to school life that zest and purpose and interest which it has lost.

One day when an express train was bearing me away from New York for a much-needed and long-anticipated holiday, a remark thrown out by a fellow passenger distracted me from my observation of the rapidly receding landscape.

"Would you believe it?" he exclaimed, "that upon a modern railroad less than eighty years old such as this, education and instruction are only just beginning to take the place of discipline and criticism? We used to suspend unsatisfactory workmen. Now we are trying to understand them and already we have far less trouble."

If the speaker had been a professor instead of a railroad official as he proceeded to tell me he was—his words would have caused me less surprise. But he had turned an unexpected searchlight upon the very problems that were then engaging my attention. As he had no idea I was an educationalist I eagerly grasped this opportunity to get an outside opinion upon them. At that moment the train flew past a band of workmen in the act of doing their job.

"Look at those men," continued my companion, "they've not the slightest idea of the best way to handle their work."

"Why not?" I inquired.

"Because the handling of the job belongs to the foreman. It is his duty to think for the gang. A labourer who thinks for himself would soon be voted a nuisance. The foreman would resent anyone telling him how to run his job and the man would probably be fired. Yet how much better the result would be if the labourer looked upon the job as his own and felt responsible for it. In that case the foreman would become a helper instead of a driver."

Our discussion ranged over station clerks, brakemen, and engineers—their training and interest in the great railroad system of which they were like cogs in the wheels. And as we talked I felt that my problem and his problem were really the same.

Finally I ventured to ask his opinion of his chief, the President of the road. The reply came in a different tone, quick with enthusiastic admiration.

"Oh! He's another sort altogether. We've a a president who knows how. He looks ahead and plans with that rare ability built up by experience. Why, when he begins to talk you soon find he's left you and your ideas as far behind as this train

has left those labourers. Yes—our president's
one in a million—a fearless human being!"

The phrase sank into my heart, for isn't that
just what we educationalists are trying to create
—*fearless human beings?* Life needs them, the
world needs them because there are never enough
to go round. They are so rare—those men and
women who can look ahead and plan—who *know
how!*

For years before that train journey I had been
asking myself whether, how, and when that kind
of fearless human being could be evolved. My
first experience of teaching came to me in a rural
school where forty pupils were divided into eight
grades or classes. I had thus to provide occupation for seven classes while I gave oral instruction to one class. To get every pupil busy on
something until I could overlook his work occurred to me as the best solution of the difficulty.
To make this plan a success I had to get the older
children to help the little ones. They, and especially the big boys, responded to my appeal. With
their assistance I transformed a storeroom into a
library. Each corner of the school room I marked
off for each different subject. In addition to the
converted storeroom, we possessed a garden and
a hall which was soon doing duty as a playroom.
Even in that stolid backwoods community no one
objected to these unconventional experiments because they were a success. The attendance rose
rapidly; the children were orderly and obedient,

and they worked with a will. Some of my popularity was due to my father, who used to tell them Indian stories when he came to fetch me every Friday. But the school authorities also showed their approval of the results attained, for at the end of the school term they reported me as "competent and of good steady habits."

Later on as instructor in a High School, Primary Schools, Normal Training Schools and a Training College I found myself up against other difficulties, and though I constantly exercised my ingenuity in seeking a solution for them I was never satisfied. It is no wonder therefore that when in 1908 a former instructor gave me a copy of Edgar James Swift's book *Mind in the Making* I was impressed by the ideas it contained.

That book influenced me and my work profoundly. I owe to it my first conception of "educational laboratories." After reading it over and over again I always returned to the two passages which seemed to contain the key to my special problems. The first ran as follows:

"The rational method is to work *with the students,* inspiring them with longing to delve into things for themselves and to make their contribution to the common fund of knowledge, to be discussed or clarified in the recitation.* The didactic method belongs to the Middle Ages. It still dominates our schools,

* Oral lesson.

though the conditions that made it serviceable have long since passed. Mental expansion of the teachers themselves is the first step towards removing this mediæval debris. *They will then investigate their pupils, the schoolroom will become an educational laboratory,* and activity will not be limited to the manual training department. *The influence of suggestion through environment has never received its proper recognition in education.* Teachers want to play a too conspicuous part in the mentations of the pupils. But the educator is limited, in the ends he may pre-elect, by the complexity of human life. *The very child whose qualities he disapproves of may be the germ of a man much beyond his own mental reach."*

To me the second passage which I quote was scarcely less illuminating. "Thus far educational experiments have been too detached and fragmentary. The few who have undertaken them were already burdened with heavy work which occupied most of their day. This left little leisure or energy for working out details or for a critical study of the results. In many instances lack of time forced the abandonment of the experiment before its completion. This is the result of failure to appreciate the importance of the work. Education has been hitherto too absorbed in its history. Teachers are constantly straining their eyes by looking over their shoulders at Pestalozzi, Froebel and Herbart, instead of looking forward to new achievements. As a result pedagogy is always on the defensive against the charge of vagueness, romanticism and particularly inadequacy. *Economy of energy is quite as truly a problem for education as for mechanics.* Efficiency —the ratio of useful work to the energy spent in accomplishing it—may be increased by lessening the resistance, or by applying more power, and teachers have occupied themselves too exclusively with producing power.''

It was Edgar Swift's book, which I gave to every student who seemed likely to understand it, that made me take the firm resolution to become a free lance in education as soon as I could, with leisure enough to experiment in the search for a new and better way.

Three years later I began to realize that ambition by drafting a plan of work for children between eight and twelve years of age to be carried out in the first ''educational laboratory.'' A colleague in a Normal Training College consented to collaborate with me while professing scepticism as to the practicability of my plan. But the fear of being condemned as a revolutionary at war against hallowed traditions prevented my discussing the new method in the classroom, though I tried to explain it outside school to a chosen band of students.

From its inception, the laboratory plan, as I

continued to call it even after perfecting it in 1913, aimed at the entire reorganization of school life. My idea was to substitute for the top-heavy machinery actually in use a simple reconstruction of school procedure under which the pupils would enjoy more freedom as well as an environment better adapted to the different sections of their studies in which each instructor should be a specialist. Above all I wanted to equalize the pupil's individual difficulties and to provide the same opportunity for advancement to the slow as to the bright child. By 1913 we had worked out the laboratory plan so as to partially eliminate the time table, but it was not until 1915 that we were able to get rid of it entirely. In 1913 we began by organizing the pupils into groups with a free choice of laboratories. That was in itself a great innovation, though they were still obliged to remain in isolated groups. It took me two years more to work out the full interaction of groups upon each other.

I was fortunate in always securing for my experiments the sympathy and encouragement of the heads of various institutions with which I was connected. My rôle of supervisor enabled me to gain experience in the problems of organization as well as in the problems of method. Of still greater value were the occasions afforded me to watch the developments of other experiments, and my petitions for leave of absence for this purpose were never refused. In 1914 I applied for per-

mission to go to Italy in order to investigate the
Montessori method. After that experience I took
part in the application of this method in Califor-
nia in 1915. On that occasion I acted as Dr. Montessori's assistant, and while a member of her
household I attended four training courses. During this period of my career I enjoyed, through the
courtesy of Dr. Frederic Burk and his interest
in my work the satisfaction of making a practical
test of my laboratory plan upon a selected group
of one hundred children, between the ages of nine
and twelve.

Between December 1915 and January 1918, having accepted the charge of looking after Dr. Montessori's interests in America, I was obliged to
abandon temporarily my experiments with the
laboratory idea. But I eagerly resumed them after
resigning this charge with the financial support
of the Child Education Foundation, which I at
that time directed. By that time I felt I had
devoted sufficient study to the individual aspect of
education. The school in its aspect of a human
society then engrossed my energy.

It was in September 1919, just fifteen years
after my first experience in teaching, that I was
able to see the laboratory plan applied in an ungraded school for crippled boys. For me it was
a great moment, and I can never be sufficiently
grateful to those who unselfishly gave me an opportunity to put my plan into practice. I might, of
course, have found other schools where the experi-

ment in its entirety could have been tried upon unhandicapped children. But both I myself and my friend, Mrs. W. Murray Crane, were actuated by the desire to give those cripples all the joy and happiness that could possibly be included in education. As trustee of that cripple school which she had helped to found and to endow, and as chairman of its Educational Committee, Mrs. W. Murray Crane deserves all the admiration I can express. Some months previously she had asked me to make any suggestions that occurred to me for the improvement of the school. It seemed to me then that the laboratory plan was just what it needed, and when in November 1918 I explained the plan to her she understood and believed in it from the very first. Some months later I visited the Cripple School and by the autumn of 1919 the plan was in operation there. Very soon it bore good fruit and aroused interest in many quarters. To me that experience was invaluable, for it was there I discovered that some device for checking progress of each pupil was a necessity. It was there I invented the Graphs which I will deal with in a later chapter. With the aid of these graphs I found it possible to simplify the organization and to perfect the interaction of the various groups.

Our success with the cripples inspired Mrs. Crane with the ambitious project of applying the laboratory plan to the boys and girls of the High School in her home town at Dalton, Massachusetts.

In February 1920 that ambition was realized. Soon after we had started on the new method, Dalton High School received the visit of Mrs. Saunderson, bringing with her Miss Belle Rennie of London, one of the pioneers of the new educational ideas in England. Miss Rennie's interest in my work led her to write about it after her return to London, and fearing that my cherished term "laboratory" might be misunderstood, I then decided to call my plan the Dalton Laboratory Plan, by which it has since been known.

I admit that the word laboratory may seem to some people inappropriate, because hitherto it has been associated exclusively with scientific experiments. But to me the word is most significant, and I cling to it advisedly in the hope that it may gradually shift the educational point of view away from the atmosphere of prejudice and moribund theories which the word "school" calls up in our minds. Let us think of school rather as a sociological laboratory where the pupils themselves are the experimenters, not the victims of an intricate and crystallized system in whose evolution they have neither part nor lot. Let us think of it as a place where community conditions prevail as they prevail in life itself.

From Dalton we went on to conquer fresh fields. I am greatly indebted to a group of friends, especially Mrs. James T. Pyle, for their faith and help in the early days. Later, through the generosity of Mr. and Mrs. W. Murray Crane, the Children's

University School was founded with the avowed object of demonstrating what the Dalton plan could do to re-vitalize education—to make it a living thing capable of arousing and preserving the interest of pupils in their work. Here it was first applied to children of pre-adolescent age. To their co-operation and to their criticism I also owe much. Even before discussing the plan in detail with my associates I presented it to the children and invited their opinion upon it. Their suggestions were extremely valuable. It was, in fact, the pupils themselves who showed me the way to correct several points in which it was defective. Thus at the very outset the principle of freedom in education for those whom we aspire to educate justified itself.

CHAPTER II

The Plan in Principle

BROADLY speaking the old type of school may be said to stand for *culture*, while the modern type of school stands for *experience*. The Dalton Laboratory Plan is primarily a way whereby both these aims can be reconciled and achieved.

The acquisition of culture is a form of experience, and as such is an element in the business of living with which school ought to be as intimately concerned as is adult existence. But it will never become so until the school as a whole is reorganized so that it can function like a community —a community whose essential condition is freedom for the individual to develop himself.

This ideal freedom is not license, still less indiscipline. It is, in fact, the very reverse of both. The child who "does as he likes" is not a free child. He is, on the contrary, apt to become the slave of bad habits, selfish and quite unfit for community life. Under these circumstances he needs some means of liberating his energy before he can grow into a harmonious, responsible being, able and willing to lend himself consciously to co-operation with his fellows for their common benefit. The Dalton Laboratory Plan provides that means by diverting his energy to the pursuit and organization of his own studies in his own way. It gives him that mental and moral liberty which we recognize as so necessary on the physical plane in order to insure his bodily well-being. Anti-social qualities and activities are, after all, merely misdirected energy.

Freedom is therefore the first principle of the Dalton Laboratory Plan. From the academic, or cultured, point of view, the pupil must be made free to continue his work upon any subject in which he is absorbed without interruption, because when interested he is mentally keener, more alert, and more capable of mastering any difficulty that may arise in the course of his study. Under the new method there are no bells to tear him away at an appointed hour and chain him pedagogically to another subject and another teacher. Thus treated, the energy of the pupil automatically runs to waste. Such arbitrary transfers are indeed as uneconomic as if we were to turn an electric stove on and off at stated intervals for no reason. Unless a pupil is permitted to absorb knowledge at his own rate of speed he will never learn anything thoroughly. Freedom is taking his own time. To take someone else's time is slavery.

The second principle of the Dalton Laboratory Plan is co-operation or, as I prefer to call it, the interaction of group life. There is a passage in Dr. John Dewey's *Democracy and Education* which admirably defines this idea. "The object of a democratic education," he writes, "is not merely to make an individual an intelligent participator in the life of his immediate group, but to bring the various groups into such constant interaction that no individual, no economic group, could presume to live independently of others."

Under the old educational system a pupil can and often does live outside his group, touching it only when he passes in company with his fellows over the common mental highway called the curriculum. This easily ends in his becoming anti-social, and if so he carries this handicap with him when he leaves school for the wider domain of life. Such a pupil may even be "an intelligent participator" in the life of his form or class, just as a teacher may be. But a democratic institution demands more than this. Real social living is more than contact; it is co-operation and interaction. A school cannot reflect the social experience which is the fruit of community life unless all its parts, or groups, develop those intimate relations one with the other and that interdependence which, outside school, binds men and nations together.

Conditions are created by the Dalton Laboratory Plan in which the pupil, in order to enjoy them, involuntarily functions as a member of a social community. He is accepted or rejected by this community according as his functioning, or conduct is social or the reverse. The law operates in school just as it does in the world of men and women. To be effective this law must not be imposed, but unwritten, an emanation as it were of the atmosphere breathed by the community. The value of community life lies in the service it renders in making each free individual composing it perpetually conscious that he, as a member, is a co-worker responsible to, and for, the whole.

This constitutes a problem in school procedure. It should be so organized that neither pupil nor teacher can isolate themselves, nor escape their due share in the activities and in the difficulties of others. We all know the teachers who hang up their personality each morning as they hang up their coats. Outside school these people have human interests and human charm which they do not dare to exhibit when with their pupils lest they should in so doing seem to abrogate their authority. The Dalton Laboratory Plan has no use for the parade of such fictitious authority, which is restrictive, not educative. Instead of promoting order it provokes indiscipline. It is fatal to the idea of a school as a vital social unit.

Equally, from the pupil's point of view, is the child when submitted to the action of arbitratory authority and to immutable rules and regulations, incapable of developing a social consciousness which is the prelude to that social experience so indispensable as a preparation for manhood and womanhood. Academically considered, the old system is just as fatal as it is from the social point of view. A child never voluntarily undertakes anything that he does not understand. The choice of his games or pursuits is determined by a clear estimate of his capabilities to excel in them. Having the responsibility of his choice his mind acts like a powerful microscope, taking in and weighing every aspect of the problem he must master in order to ensure success. Given the same free conditions his mind would act on the problems of study in exactly the same way. Under the Dalton Laboratory Plan we place the work problem squarely before him, indicating the standard which has to be attained. After that he is allowed to tackle it as he thinks fit in his own way and at his own speed. Responsibility for the result will develop not only his latent intellectual powers, but also his judgment and character.

But in order that he may accomplish this educative process—in order that he may be led to educate himself—we must give him an opportunity to survey the whole of the task we set. To win the race he must first get a clear view of the goal. It would be well to lay a whole twelvemonth's work before the pupil at the beginning of the school year. This will give him a perspective of the plan of his education. He will thus be able to judge of the steps he must take each month and each week so that he may cover the whole road, instead of going blindly forward with no idea either of the road or the goal. How so handicapped can a child be expected to be interested in the race even to desire to win it? How can a teacher hope to turn out a well-equipped human being unless he takes the trouble to study the psychology of the child? Both for master and for pupil a perception of their job is essential. Education is, after all, a co-operative task. Their success or failure in it is interlocked.

Children learn, if we would only believe it, just as men and women learn, by adjusting means to ends. What does a pupil do when given, as he is given by the Dalton Laboratory Plan, responsibility for the performance of such and such work? Instinctively he seeks the best way of achieving it. Then having decided, he proceeds to act upon that decision. Supposing his plan does not seem to fit his purpose, he discards it and tries another. Later on he may find it profitable to consult his fellow students engaged in a similar task. Discussion helps to clarify his ideas and also his plan of procedure. When he comes to the end the finished achievement takes on all the splendour of success. It embodies all he has thought and felt and lived during the time it has taken to complete. This is real experience. It is culture acquired through individual development and through collective co-operation. It is no longer school—it is life.

Not only will this method of education stimulate the deepest interest and the highest powers in a student, but it will teach him how to proportion effort to attainment. In his book upon the principles of war General Foch says: "Economy of forces consists in throwing all the forces at one's disposition at a given time upon one point." So the child's attack upon his problem of work should be facilitated by allowing him to concentrate all his forces upon the subject that claims his interest at one particular moment. He will in this case not only do more work, but better work too. The Dalton Laboratory Plan permits pupils to budget their time and to spend it according to their need.

"The secret of education," so Emerson tells us, "lies in respecting the pupil. It is not for you to chose what he shall know, what he shall do. It is chosen and fore-ordained and he alone holds the key to his own secret. By your tampering and thwarting and too much governing he may be hindered from his end and kept out of his own. Respect the child. Wait and see the new product of nature. Nature loves analogies but not repetitions. Respect the child. Be not too much his parent. Trespass not on his solitude.

"But I hear the outcry which replies to this suggestion: Would you verily throw up the reins of public and private discipline; would you leave the young child to the mad career of his own passions and whimsies and call this anarchy respect for the child's nature? I answer: Respect the child, respect him to the end, but also respect yourself. Be the companion of his thought, the friend of his friendship, the lover of his virtue, but no kinsman of his sin. He makes wild attempts to explain himself, and invokes the aid and consent of the bystanders. Baffled by want of language and methods to convey his meaning, not yet clear to himself, he conceives that though not in this house or town, yet in some other house or town is the wise master who can put him in possession of the rules and instruments to execute his will. Happy this child with a bias, with a thought which entrances him, leads him, now into deserts, now into cities, the fool of an idea. Let him follow it in good and evil report, in good or in bad company. It will justify itself; it will lead him at last into that illustrious society of the lovers of truth.

"Cannot we let people be themselves and enjoy life in their own way? You are trying to make that man another you. One's enough.

"Or we sacrifice the genius of the pupil, the unknown possibilities of his nature, to a weak and safe uniformity as the Turks whitewash the costly mosaics of ancient art which the Greeks left on their temple walls. Rather let us have men whose manhood is only the continuation of their boyhood, natural character still: such are able and fertile for heroic action; and not that sad spectacle with which we are too familiar, educated eyes in uneducated bodies.

"I like boys, the masters of the playground and the street—boys who have the same liberal ticket of admission to all shops, factories, armouries,

town-meetings, caucuses, mobs, target-shootings
as flies have; quite unsuspected, coming in as naturally as the janitor—known to have no money in
their pockets, and themselves not suspecting the
value of this poverty; putting nobody on his
guard, but seeing the inside of the show—hearing
all the sides. There are no secrets from them,
they know everything that befalls in the fire company, the merits of every engine and of every man
at the brakes, how to work it, and are swift to
try their hand on every part; so, too, the merits
of every locomotive on the rails, and will coax
the engineers to let them ride with him and pull
the handles when it goes into the engine-house.
They are there only for fun, and not knowing that
they are at school, in the court-house, or the cattle
show quite as much and more than they were, an
hour ago, in the arithmetic class.

"They know truth from counterfeit as quick
as the chemist does. They detect weakness in your
eye and behaviour a week before you open your
mouth, and have given you the benefit of their
opinion quick as a wink. They make no mistakes,
have no pedantry, but entire belief in experience."

It is just that experience, individual and social,
which the Dalton Laboratory Plan aspires to provide within the school walls. The principles out-
lined in Emerson's picturesque prose are its principles. It shows the way, and I firmly believe
the only way, to make school as attractive, and as
educative as play, and ultimately to create those

fearless human beings which, understood in the widest sense, is our ideal.

But as liberty is an integral part of that ideal I have carefully guarded against the temptation to make my plan a stereotyped cast-iron thing ready to fit any school anywhere. So long as the principle that animates it is preserved, it can be modified in practice in accordance with the circumstances of the school and the judgment of the staff. For this reason I refrain from dogmatizing on what subjects should be included in the curriculum, or by what standards the achievement of pupils should be measured. Above all, I do not want to canalize the life-blood of citizenship. On this point I can but say that the curriculum of any school should vary according to the needs of the pupils, and even in schools where it is designed to serve a definite academic purpose, this aspect should not be lost sight of as it often is. Until the educational world wakes to the fact that curriculum is not the chief problem of society, we shall, I fear, continue to handicap our youth by viewing it through the wrong end of the telescope.

To-day we think too much of curricula and too little about the boys and girls. The Dalton Plan is not a panacea for academic ailments. It is a plan through which the teacher can get at the problem of child psychology and the pupil at the problem of learning. It diagnoses school situations in terms of boys and girls. Subject difficulties concern students, not teachers. The curriculum is but our technique, a means to an end. The instrument to be played upon is the boy or girl.

Under the conditions that exist in the average school the energies of these boys and girls cannot flow freely. The top-heavy organization has been built up for the instructor, and with it teachers are expected to solve their problems. But I contend that the real problem of education is not a teacher's but a pupil's problem. All the difficulties that harass the teacher are created by the unsolved difficulties of the pupils. When the latter disappear the former will vanish also, but not before the school organization and its attendant machinery has been re-made for the pupil, who is rendered inefficient and irritable by being compelled to use a mechanism that is not his own.

The first thing, therefore, is to remove all impediments that prevent the pupil from getting at his problem. Only he knows what his real difficulties are, and unless he becomes skilled in dispersing them he will become skilled in concealing them. Hitherto our educational system has been content to tap the surface water of his energy. Now we must try to reach and release the deep well of his natural powers. In doing so we shall assist and encourage the expression of his lifeforce and harness it to the work of education. This is not to be achieved by doing the pupil's work for him, but by making it possible for him to do his own work. Harmony between teacher and pupil is

essential if we would avoid those emotional conflicts which are the most distracting among the ills
the old type of school is heir to.

Experience of the Dalton Laboratory Plan
shows, moreover, that it is beneficial to the pupils
morally as well as mentally. Where it is put into
operation conflicts cease, disorder disappears.
The resistance generated in the child by the old
inelastic machinery to the process of learning is
transformed into acquiescence, and then into
interest and industry as soon as he is released to
carry out the educational programme in his own
way. Freedom and responsbility together perform the miracle.

Briefly summarized, the aim of the Dalton Plan
is a synthetic aim. It suggests a simple and economic way by means of which the school as a whole
can function as a community. The conditions under which the pupils live and work are the chief
factors of their environment, and a favourable
environment is one which provides opportunities
for spiritual as well as mental growth. It is the
social experience accompanying the tasks, not
the tasks themselves, which stimulates and fur-
thers both these kinds of growth. Thus the
Dalton Plan lays emphasis upon the importance
of the child's living while he does his work, and
the manner in which he acts as a member of society, rather than upon the subjects of his curriculum. It is the sum total of these twin expe-

riences which determines his character and his knowledge.

As illustrating this line of thought I cannot do better than cite a passage from Miss Emily Wilson's book entitled *An Experiment in Synthetic Education.** It is a little book which contains a big message.

"The main subjects of our curriculum must be taught synthetically—that is, in their relation to each other—and not in self-contained compartments. Only in the synthetic way, only by realizing and constantly emphasizing that to know something of Man we must study and correlate his History, his environment, his Science, Literature and Art, can we make knowledge a living and fruitful organism rather than a dead and barren file. . . .

"It is necessary to emphasize a fact not sufficiently appreciated; it is easier to learn at the same time two subjects that have living relationships with one another than to learn one subject which is represented as an isolated fact having no vital relationship with anything else. Pure memory work is difficult and a burden to the mind. The moment the annual examinations are over we forget, never to recall, those unrelated facts with which we crammed our youthful brains. But once a relation is established as between one subject and another, both those subjects in so far as

* Quotation made by permission of the publishers.

they are alive, that is are related, are retained with perfect ease. . . .

"That this consciousness of the inter-relation of all subjects cannot fail to bear good fruit in the field of ethics and religion will be obvious. For service and co-operation are what we need to solve our great political and social problems to-day, and synthetic education that will provide that large and comprehensive outlook which will make these virtues a habit of thought and a practice of life. Some such total vision must be constantly in the mind of the teacher, who must ever be on the look-out for inter-relations and so stir within the minds of the children the faculty of creating channels between the different territories; channels which will fertilize the whole earth between them and give that infinite joy which comes from the consciousness of creatorship, the true function of man, the work for which he was endowed with an immortal spirit."

From the parent's point of view the principles of the Dalton Plan are admirably epitomized in a letter recently contributed to the *New York Evening Post* by the parent of two pupils attending the Children's University School.

To the Editor of the *New York Evening Post:*
The Dalton Laboratory Plan is a decided novelty. Its adoption in England before we New Yorkers even heard about it shows how

much more popular is the subject of education over there than here.

As a parent of two children I wish to urge a more widespread acquaintance with the methods worked out in the Dalton Plan. It diagnoses the child's dislike for his studies as not due to the studies themselves, but to the methods used in teaching him. It does not start out with the belief that the child has an innate dislike for study. It is the fault of the educational process to which he is forced to submit which embitters his young soul against any or all subjects indiscriminately. The Dalton Plan is not an arbitrary process imposed on the child without regard to his aptitude, but is an enlistment of the child's own interest in his acquisition of knowledge. The Dalton Plan elicits a new response from the child's nature by inviting him to undertake the job in a way that appeals to his natural desire to learn things in his own way and even in his own time. The teacher gives him the same friendly help and encouragement to master his problems that one adult would give to another in the course of business or any undertaking of life, but the child is embarked on an adventure into the realms of knowledge with his own standard flying at the peak and his own command of his resources.

There is such a thing as culture. We treasure it as the embodiment of our civilization and we know that the stability of our social life depends upon the majority of our young people getting at least the elements of that culture. The Dalton Plan points a way to make the process natural and spontaneous rather than forced and arbitrary. It evokes in the child a spirit of self-reliance and initiative and so starts his character building at once. Here is life experience for the little fellow. He studies on his own responsibility in the company of his fellows, all pursuing the same adventure. He forms the same kind of relationships in his school life that he will afterwards get in his business or professional life. He is learning by trying. He is not struggling under constant direction and restraint. He is part of the real life of the world, sharing its problems, realizing the emptiness of idleness, and enjoying the rewards of industry. There is nothing false or artificial in these relationships. But, most important of all, the Dalton Plan starts him out on this basis full ten or fifteen years ahead of the boy or girl who is now going through the treadmill of our day schools.

CHAPTER III

The Plan in Practice

I come now to a consideration of the Dalton Laboratory Plan in its practical application to the problem of education. Perhaps in order to clear the ground it is well to begin by indicating what it is not.

The Dalton Laboratory Plan is not a system or a method, which through ages of use has petrified into a monotonous and uniform shape, to be branded on to succeeding generations of pupils as sheep are branded on going into a fold. It is not a curriculum, which, all too often, is simply the machine by means of which the brand is stamped upon the individuals caught in the meshes of the system. Practically speaking, it is a scheme of educational reorganization which reconciles the twin activities of teaching and learning. When intelligently applied it creates conditions which enable the teacher to teach and the learner to learn.

In order to apply the scheme it is not necessary or even desirable to abolish classes or forms as units of organization in the school, nor the curriculum as such. The Dalton Laboratory Plan preserves both. Each pupil is classified as a member of a form, and for each form a maximum and a minimum curriculum is drawn up. But at its inception it lays the whole work proposition before the pupils in the shape of a contract job. The curriculum is divided up into jobs and the pupil accepts the work assigned for his class as a contract. Though dispensed with above middle school, the younger children may sign a definite contract which is returned to each individual as soon as his job is completed.

"I ——, pupil of —— standard form, contract to do the —— assignment.

Date and signature ——."

As every month of the year has its own assigned work, a contract-job for any one form comprises a whole month's work. For convenience we arrange the different parts of the curriculum under the heading of major and minor subjects:

MAJOR SUBJECTS.	MINOR SUBJECTS.
Mathematics	Music
History	Art
Science	Handiwork
English	Domestic Science
Geography	Manual Training
Foreign Languages, etc.	Gymnastics, etc.

The first category of subjects is not more important than the other, but they are classified as "major" because they are used as the basis of promotion in most schools, and college entrance examinations thus necessitate that more time should be given to them. The value of the minor subjects lies in their expansive influence upon the student. The study of them creates a response to beauty and also an increased power of expression. But if in the lower school, which includes children ranging from eight to twelve years, foreign languages are not required as a basis for promotion, they should be classified as minor subjects for lower-school pupils.

For the purpose of simplifying the initial application of the Dalton Laboratory Plan, I recommend that it should be applied firstly to major subjects alone. As the new scheme becomes familiar it can gradually be extended to the minor subjects. Take, for example, a school wherein the major subjects for Form II are Mathematics, Science, History, Geography, English, and French. The first contract-job for a pupil belonging to that form would be a block of the year's curriculum comprising a month's work in each of these major subjects. In the United States we reckon a school month as twenty days. The contract would therefore cover the ground divided as below:

TWENTY DAYS

Form II Contract Job

1 month of French	1 month of English	1 month of Science	1 month of Mathematics	1 month of Geography	1 month of History

This diagram represents a required standard of work for the performance of which each pupil in Form II would contract. Though the standard is the same, the pupils are not. As their mental legs must be of different lengths, their rate of speed in study must vary also. Some may not even need the twenty days for their contracted work; others may not be able to get it done in that time. It is of the essence of the Dalton Laboratory Plan that pupils should progress each at his own rate, for only so can the work be assimilated thoroughly. Thus each pupil must be allowed to organize his method of working as he thinks best. Unfortunately at the outset we cannot assume that these pupils know how to work, though as the new plan is put into operation they will gradually learn to organize both their time and work to better and better advantage. But efficiency means speed, and speed will only be attained when good habits of work are established. It takes time to counteract the habit of dependence bred in the pupil by constantly telling him what to do, when and how to do it. This system made him a servant, occasionally an efficient servant, but always dependent on orders. And though the reorganization of school machinery is quickly effected the response of the pupil to the changed conditions is not always as rapid. It is the business of the teacher to see that the adjustment proceeds, however, slowly. The process can be helped by making the divided curriculum clear, and by

seeing that the pupil grasps the whole scope and
nature of the work he contracts to accomplish.
Unless he understands what is required of him
his organization of his time will be defective.

By giving his task in the form of a contract for
whose execution he feels himself responsible, we
give the work dignity and him the consciousness of a definite purpose. This feeling is increased if we make him aware of our confidence
in his desire and in his power to execute it. A
pupil must not, however, be permitted to continue
the study of any major subject beyond the limits
of the month's assignment unless he has completed
his contract in every subject. He must not be allowed to work up to a higher standard than his
form average in one or two subjects and fall below
it in the rest of them. This would merely give
him an opportunity of evading progress in those
studies in which he is weak and lose to him the
value of correlated and vitalized subjects. Uniformity of standard insures that he will so organize his time that most of it will be devoted to
overcome his individual weaknesses and difficulties. The plan teaches him to *budget his time* so
that it is sufficient to his needs and to have him go
slowly and thoroughly. In this way he will be
well prepared for each succeeding step. His subject diet will be well balanced and his culture will
be well rounded.

The amount of any monthly assignment is a
part and a very vital part of the teacher's prob-

lem. A good curriculum should be so balanced and co-related that neither too much nor too little is included in the contract-job. In the lower school not more should be required than the pupils can easily accomplish by a wise division of their time. That a ten-year-old child should learn all that a normal child of his age can learn is the ideal to set before us. A study of child psychology is necessary if we are to reorganize the machinery of education so that it corresponds to his powers and satisfies his needs at every age.

Turning from the pupil to the school building, it is evident that the Dalton Laboratory Plan exacts the establishment of laboratories, one for each subject in the curriculum, though with a small teaching staff two subjects may be studied in a single laboratory. A specialist in that particular subject, or subjects, should be in charge of each laboratory whose relation to the scheme I will deal with later on. For the moment I want to emphasize the point that these laboratories are the places where the children experiment—where they are free to work on their jobs, not places where they are experimented upon.

The text-book library of the school must be distributed among these laboratories according to subject. It is of course essential that the necessary books should be always accessible to every student—a supply of scientific books in the science laboratory, history books in the history laboratory, and so on. With regard to these books, it is well to have a few standard text-books and to increase as far as possible the number of reference books. Do not be afraid of including in the school library books that are designed for adult readers, the kind of books which have hitherto been found rather on home, than on school, bookshelves. Remember that no book can be too well written to interest a child. The dry terseness of the ordinary school manual, devoid of any literary quality, is responsible for half the distaste of learning so characteristic of the average school boy or girl. It is at school that our future men and women should become acquainted with those literary treasures which are the common heritage of humanity. And regarded merely as a mine of information, nothing could be more valuable in the development of the pupil's intelligence than the opportunity thus given him of comparing the different views of different authors on the subject he is studying.

Among the impediments to true education which is ruthlessly abolished by the Dalton Laboratory Plan is the time-table. Even to the teacher the time-table is a bugbear. How often have I heard head masters and mistresses complain of the difficulty of dividing time so that no member of the teaching staff should feel his special subjects slighted! As a result the time-table is usually compiled rather in the interest of the instructors than of the pupils. To the latter the time-table is nothing less than a curse. Its banishment is in fact the first step towards his liberation.

Let us assume that in a given school laboratory time for all classes or forms extends from 9 to 12 o'clock every morning. Under the Dalton Plan this three-hour period is devoted to the study of the major subjects—Geography, History, Mathematics, Science, English, and French. Before setting out to organize their time themselves each pupil consults his teacher, who, under the new plan, has become a subject specialist, or adviser. Together they go over the pupil's contract work, classifying his subjects as strong and weak. Those subjects which a child loves and enjoys studying will usually be found among his strong subjects. The subjects he is weak in are almost invariably those which he finds difficult to understand and assimilate, chiefly because he has not hitherto been able to give enough time to them.

For the sake of clarity I will take a concrete example. Mary Smith is a member of Form II. When, with the aid of her adviser, she has sorted out her subjects, we will suppose that they fall into the two following categories:

WEAK SUBJECTS.	STRONG SUBJECTS.
Mathematics	English
French	History
	Geography
	Science

In relation to the three hours' laboratory time at her disposal we may express her individual needs by the following equation:

THREE HOURS' LABORATORY TIME

$$\underset{\text{(Weak Subjects)}}{\text{Mathematics+French}} = \underset{\text{(Strong Subjects)}}{\text{English+History+Geography+Science}}$$

Having accepted her contract-job she must keep the whole job in mind, and being weak in French and Mathematics she needs to devote as much time to them as to her four strong subjects. But if the time-table were in force, Mary, despite her difficulties, would only be allowed as long for her Mathematics and French as the other pupils in Form II, many of whom might be strong in them. Can a more complete condemnation of the time-table be found than this simple demonstration of its working?

Emancipated from its tyranny, Mary's equation will change as she eliminates antipathy to, or weakness in, those subjects. But as long as her problem can be expressed in the terms of the above equation, she should devote half of her three available hours every day to Mathematics and French, and only the remaining half to the other four subjects. If she is stronger in French than in Mathematics then the one-and-one-half hours should be divided accordingly.

Mary, will, however, be free to choose which subject she will take up first, and she will go into the laboratory consecrated to that subject. Having chosen it at the moment when her interest in it is keen, she will do better work and do it more quickly too. Once in the laboratory Mary proceeds to study as an individual, but if she finds other members from Form II there she works with them. This is the rule of the laboratory under the Dalton Plan. It subdivides and reduces the large class group and it creates a small group of pupils doing intensive work, which stimulates discussion and exercises social influence. The educative value of such small groups is immense in giving an atmosphere to the laboratory, in providing occasions for social adjustment and experience. It provides invaluable play of mind upon mind. As Mary has entered that laboratory voluntarily, and can leave it for another when she feels inclined, no problems of discipline arise. Her mind comes in with her and goes out with her, disciplined by interest in the subject, harnessed—the whole of it—to her job. No time is wasted, for though the general time-table has gone Mary has, in consultation with her adviser, made a time-table for herself. This is very important, especially in the case of the younger children, in order to inculcate the value of time. To spend it in supplying our mental and moral needs is to put it to the wisest use.

It is also essential to Mary that she should realize exactly what progress she is making in the subject of her choice. For this purpose I invented the graph device before alluded to. As it merits a chapter to itself I will only now refer to it casually as a part of the laboratory equipment and procedure. There are three sets of graphs. The first provides each special teacher and adviser with the means of following the individual progress of each pupil, and of comparing it with that of the other members of the class. It also enables the pupil himself to compare his progress with that of his classmates. But Mary has also her own contract-job graph, on which she records her daily progress. The third graph pictures the progress of the class or form a whole, as well as the individual progress.

So that the pupil should never lose sight of the job in its entirety, progress is measured in weeks of work accomplished. Mary has six major subjects with four weeks of work on each of them. Her contract thus entails twenty-four weeks of work. On the weekly graph she is therefore marked, not in each separate subject, but in the number of weeks' work done out of the total required, week by week.

In this manner a pupil advances steadily, job by job, through the curriculum of his class. If in a school year of nine or ten months he only finishes eight jobs on account of absence or illness, he begins the ninth job in the following year. The clever child may, on the contrary, accomplish in one year the work mapped out to cover eighteen months. Often the slow, apparently less intelligent, child gains in rapidity, and in any case he builds well and soundly at his own natural rate.

CHAPTER IV

Its Application—A Concrete Example

THE Dalton Laboratory Plan can be applied to the reorganization of any school with the exception of infant or primary schools designed for children under nine years of age. Above that limit we classify schools in the United States into lower, middle, and upper, but as I am writing mainly for British readers I shall use the terms "elementary" and "secondary" in the English sense when alluding to English schools. In America an elementary school is a lower school, ordinarily consisting of fourth to eighth grades inclusive, and may be private or public, that is, paying or free. With us, public schools are invariably free schools supported out of public funds, not, as in the case of Eton and Harrow, open only to pupils whose parents are able to pay for their tuition.

As a general rule the Dalton Plan is applied as an efficiency measure for the purpose of accomplishing a programme of work already standardized for the different forms or grades. It is susceptible, however, of a much greater extension in the direction of our ideal in education, as some day I hope it will be, by being applied to the organization of a new venture instead of the reorganization of an old one. In this case it could be used for the carrying out of a freer curriculum composed entirely of projects set by the pupils themselves, and where the instructors would be regarded as consultant specialists.

At the moment, however, I shall confine my observations to its application as an efficiency measure involving both academic and social reorganization. In this connection I must again insist upon the necessity of bearing always in mind that my plan or "way" connotes not only a change of curriculum or method, but a change in the whole life and spirit of the school. This socialization of the school, as I call it, is as vital to the success of the experiment as is the liberation of the pupil.

As a concrete illustration of my meaning I will describe the initiation of the Dalton Laboratory Plan in a lower school, dealing first with the academic aspect of the question. In this school there were one hundred and fifty children ranging in age from nine to thirteen. They were classified in five grades, fourth to eighth inclusive, with thirty pupils in each grade. This school was a free public school. Had it been private and paying the classes would certainly have been smaller.

These five grades occupied five rooms, each grade being in charge of a regular form, or grade teacher. Mathematics, History, Geography, English, and Science being considered the major subjects, or "tools of knowledge," were taught in each grade. They were the standardized fundamentals and were, moreover, regarded as the basis of promotion. French, Music, Art, Gymnastics, Needlework, and Cooking were considered minor subjects, but after the adoption of the plan French became a major subject. Before that time the major subjects received daily attention in oral lessons, the minor ones several times a week, though music was in a way a daily task as the children usually inaugurated the school hours with singing. Practically the whole morning was given up to the first category of subjects, while the afternoon was reserved for the second. Subsequently, music and art were put upon a laboratory basis, and full-time, instead of twice-weekly, instructors, were engaged to teach them.

For some time the Dalton Laboratory Plan had been under discussion when one day the principal called the five form mistresses to a conference on the matter. These mistresses were just average teachers, neither more nor less intelligent than the majority in their profession. Their observations disclosed varying degrees of dissatisfaction with the working of the old system. Several of them agreed that its demand that each instructor should be an expert in the teaching of every subject in the curriculum was inclined to make them jack-of-all-trades and masters of none. All of them testified to the constant, and often insuperable, difficulty of arousing the interest of the pupils in their lessons. Much class-time was wasted in overcoming their disinclination to proceed with the scheduled business of the day. One teacher rather pathetically described her efforts to dramatize the lesson in the hope of interesting the children. After searching the library to get up the subject she would often spend the night in preparing to present it in a thrilling and exciting manner. Her subject was history, and she related how she had once tried to win the attention of the children with a romantic account of the French-Indian war. But her only reward for all this expenditure of energy was an appeal from one of the children for information regarding the North Pole and Eskimos, suggested probably by the snow that was then falling outside the school windows!

Similar experiences were detailed by other teachers. The impossibility of adjusting the character of the lesson and its length to pupils whose capacity for absorption varied from child to child, was also cited as a defect in the system by all the teachers in unison. It was usually too short for the alert pupil to whom the subject was easy, and who was consequently quick at the up-take. It was too long for the child whose mind had flown out of the window after something about which he was naturally enthusiastic, and far too long for the slow-minded pupil who needed much explanation and who grasped ideas slowly. Even those among the teachers who considered themselves good disciplinarians acknowledged that, though able to control the bodies of their pupils, the soul almost invariably escaped their authority.

A series of questions put by the principal elicited the fact that every one of the teachers had a favourite subject which she would like to teach all the time, while several added that the effort to impart knowledge on a variety of subjects was totally disproportionate to the result achieved with their pupils. It is not surprising that under these circumstances all five mistresses received with relief and joy the announcement that the old unsatisfactory system was to be abandoned. They were then told that the school was to be reorganized on the Dalton Laboratory Plan, under which each instructor would be able to devote all her energy to teaching her best subject and only that. Every one of the old grade rooms was henceforth to be converted into a laboratory where pupils belonging to all grades would come to study that one particular subject with the help of the teacher who adopted it.

The next step was the rearrangement of school equipment preliminary to the initiation of the new plan. All the geographical apparatus books, maps, and globes were concentrated in one room, the surplus above what would in future be required demonstrating the superiority of the Dalton Plan from the point of view of economy. The same transportation was effected of all the tools pertaining to the study of the other subjects, and lastly the library was distributed among the laboratories upon the same principle. Already it was evident that the vitalizing process had begun. A new spirit seemed to prevail among the teachers which made them friends on a new plane instead of rivals. Each realized she would have, in future, a definite and sympathetic domain in which her interests would not clash with those of any of her colleagues. Of course there were some misgivings; some half-expressed fears of failure when the great innovation should be put to the acid test of practice. What would happen, some of them wondered, if certain pupils known for their ingenuity in bringing the most promising schemes of teachers to naught should set out to wreck the new experiment? But to all these doubts and anticipations of evil the principal opposed her cheerful optimism. She had faith in the miracle and declared it. Once in operation the resistance of the children would, she was convinced, fade like frost in June. "Change the conditions," she repeated, "and you change the pressure. Change the pressure and you will change the product."

The fact that in this school the decision to adopt the Dalton Laboratory Plan was taken at the end of the term made the necessary time available to prepare both materially and psychologically. When the old classroom desks were re-grouped in the laboratories they were placed front to front, five together, to make tables for the use of the

separate grade groups. In order to facilitate
adjustment to the new organization these latter
were numbered 4, 5, 6, 7, 8 to indicate the different
grade groups that were to use them. Coloured
cards corresponding to the numbers were chosen to
designate the different grades, and also the individual graphs for the checking of progress. In
the hall one hundred and fifty lockers were erected
and numbered to serve as a receptacle where each
pupil could keep the miscellaneous articles which
formerly accumulated in the classroom desk.
Finally, the art mistress provided each of her colleagues with a sign card that was fixed to the door
of each laboratory to indicate the subject. Just
outside a notice board was placed to carry grade
assignments; inside there was a similar board
destined for laboratory graphs. The conversion
of a store-room into a staff-room—which till then,
had been entirely lacking—with its own notice
board completed the transformation scene.

The following simple diagram will show what
the transformation from one teacher with many
subjects to one teacher with one subject meant to
the staff.

Miss A:	4th Grade	Math.	5 Gr.	Math.	6 Gr.	Math.	7 Gr.	Math.	8 Gr.	Math.
Miss B:	"	Eng.	"	Eng.	"	Eng.	"	Eng.	"	Eng.
Miss C:	"	Hist.	"	Hist.	"	Hist.	"	Hist.	"	Hist.
Miss D:	"	Geog.	"	Geog.	"	Geog.	"	Geog.	"	Geog.
Miss E:	"	Science	"	Sci.	"	Sci.	"	Sci.	"	Sci.

With regard to the important question of assignment the average capacity of each grade was
carefully considered in order to determine the

amount of work which ought to be required from
the pupils of each of the five grades during a
school month of twenty days. This investigation
revealed the enormous amount of work which had
been set, and made the teachers realize how "over-
padded" the assignments were. A process of cutting down was then resorted to. Departmental
cuts were effected between departments by agreement, by crediting the pupils with a certain scale
of work already fulfilled. Academic cuts reduced
the amount of subject matter. When completed,
these assignments were attached to coloured cards
corresponding to the grade colours and hung on
the notice boards outside the laboratories. Outside
the history laboratory all the history assignments
for the five grades were hung, and so on. On the
notice boards inside the laboratories correspond-
ingly coloured laboratory graphs were fixed for
recording individual progress.

A detailed exposition of the Dalton Laboratory
Plan was given to each teacher for study during
the holidays. When the pupils assembled at the
beginning of the next term the principal gave them
a simple explanation of the changes that had been
made in the organization of their work, and
showed them how the contract cards and graphs
were to be used. They were told that the time-
tables and the class-bell had been abolished; that
henceforward they were free to enter any laboratory quietly without asking permission, and to
work there on any subject as long as they desired.

The three hours, from 9 to 12, would now be considered as their own time for the use of which they were individually responsible. It was to be budgeted according to the difficulties each subject presented to each pupil. It was explained that they would be checked academically according to their progress towards fulfillment of the contracted job, and socially according to the way in which they "shouldered the job." At 12 o'clock the fourth grade were told to report to Miss A in the mathematic laboratory. She would then and thereafter once each week, give them an oral lesson in mathematics. Similarly, the fifth grade was to report to Miss B; the sixth to Miss C; the seventh to Miss D; and the eighth to Miss E. This first assignment to oral lessons began for each grade with the subject specialist who acted also as the advisor for a particular grade or class. The social and ethical aspects of the Dalton Laboratory Plan were not alluded to on that occasion. This side of the new method was first discussed with the parents and subsequently with the pupils themselves.

Although somewhat confused about it all, the interest of the children in the new scheme was immediately evident. In order to help its initiation on that very first morning the principal assigned groups to the various laboratories. As there were thirty pupils in each grade, she assigned six pupils from each grade, making thirty in all, to each of the subject laboratories for further instruction in the scheme from the mistress who was awaiting their arrival.

On account of what happened in Miss D's laboratory may be taken as typical of the events of the morning in all the other laboratories. Each group was isolated together round the cluster of desks which had been set apart for each grade. The grade assignments from the outside notice boards were distributed among the groups, one pupil in each reading it quietly to the rest, while Miss D went from one to another offering suggestions and giving assistance. Notebooks were then distributed to each pupil, one for each subject, which were either to be left in the laboratory or kept in the locker. After the entire assignment had been read copies of it were distributed for the general use of each group with instructions to leave them in a portfolio upon the grade-tables or desks. The time had now come when they were told to start work and to communicate either with a member of their group or with their teacher in case they desired help. Without communication intimate discussion and play of mind upon mind would have been impossible. The laboratory would have become a mere study hall, not an interacting stimulating society. When any pupil had finished any portion of the first week's assignment he was told that he might leave that laboratory and go into any other he preferred after recording on his own and on the grade-graph the amount of work done.

Within twenty minutes the pupils had grasped the outline of the organization and had settled down to study. As each became absorbed in the subject the room grew almost silent, or as Miss D afterwards expressed it, "one felt an atmosphere growing there of real, contented work." At intervals during the morning one pupil after another finished a piece of work and was asked by Miss D where he would then like to go. This question was only necessary that first morning in order to ensure that the pupil had really decided what subject he would take up next, and also to give him ballast and encouragement. If wavering, he was asked to remain until he could come to a real decision. As pupils came into the laboratory from others, Miss D greeted them as one would greet a guest, for it is essential to remove any feeling of restraint or embarrassment. Fortunately, the old nagging and driving on one hand and sullen resistance on the other had already vanished.

At 12 o'clock each grade reported, as arranged, to its assigned laboratory, where the mistress gave them an oral lesson lasting 45 minutes on some one subject, and handed them the weekly schedule of these lessons in which a different subject was to be treated each day. These lessons were now called "conferences" because the entire class, who had been working in separate laboratories, individually or in small voluntary groups, now met to confer over the problems of their assignment. At these conferences they compared progress, brought up and discussed their special difficulties, and helped to solve the difficulties of their fellow pupils. The greatest keenness was shown at these conferences; the discussions were genuine and really helpful to all concerned. Each conference was social because the school itself had been socialized by the plan.

The Subject Supervisors who paid weekly visits to the school showed an intense interest in the working of the new plan. It made it possible for a supervisor visiting the school at any time during the morning to see in her subject laboratory the study in full swing. By examining the assignments she could easily check subject content. Instead of spending much of her time in advising teachers how to discipline and control their classes, the Dalton Plan enabled her to discuss and correlate the work in company with other supervisors and the teachers. At the same time a single librarian could spend a few days each month in a single school and go from laboratory to laboratory to arrange for the care and the exchange of books.

Subsequent mornings, weeks, and months only served to confirm the success of the first trial of the new organization. And gradually under its influence learning did indeed become as much a pleasure as play.

CHAPTER V

Assignments—How to Make Them

It is not too much to say that the Dalton Laboratory Plan hinges upon the assignment; for on the degree of skill and understanding with which it is compiled, the successful application of the new plan will largely depend. Its importance will be appreciated when we remember that the pupil can only reach a complete survey of the work expected of him through the medium of each separate assigment. Collectively considered, they represent an outline of the contract-job in all its parts.

Though the adjustment of the work to be done to the capacity of the pupils has always constituted the chief problem of a teacher, sufficient attention has not hitherto been devoted to it from the point of view of the individual pupil. All too frequently the preparation set has merely required the study of a certain number of pages in a text-book or manual, and often this requirement has been hurled at the pupil at the end of a class period after his attention has already been claimed from another class by the pre-dismissal gong. Under these circumstances it is no wonder that the child fails to grasp the exact meaning of the hastily fixed assignment, and even its relation to the subject in hand.

The first condition of a good assignment is that it shall be invariably written, not oral, clearly expressed, and designed to show the pupil what it is leading up to. In drawing it up the teacher must get rid of the idea that she is preparing a plan for herself. What is needed is a plan to be used by the pupils as a guide in their attack upon the parts of their contract-job. A good assignment represents a block of the whole job compiled from the standpoint of the pupil himself.

Few children at any age know instinctively how to work. As the object of the Dalton Plan is primarily to teach them this, the instructor should be careful at the outset not to demand too much. Versatility, resourcefulness, and general efficiency will be better developed if the whole contract is proportionate to the mental power of the average child. On no account should it surpass his capacity to grasp it as a whole. He must be able to take it in before he can measure his time wisely and set himself to its consistent accomplishment. Only the job which he feels to be within his reach will stimulate the growth of his interest, and ultimately of his creative powers.

In cases where experience has revealed a marked disparity of intelligence between the pupils of the same age and form, it is sometimes well to modify the assignment in order to bring it within the reach of, say, three different categories. The minimum assignment will merely require the essentials for a form foundation, and its execution should not put too great a strain upon the least gifted pupils in the class. The medium assignment would be given to the next group of moderately intelligent children, while the maximum assignment would be reserved for the star pupils. As any individual gained ground or developed intellectually, which is a common phenomenon after the Dalton Plan has been in operation for some time, he could be moved from the minimum to the maximum group. But it should never be forgotten that uniformity is not at all synonymous with progress.

At the start one month's contract will give the student a sufficient perspective, and even this should be divided up into weekly allotments, so that the pupil should be able to mark his own progress, step by step, as he goes on. In so doing he will gain the satisfaction of so much accomplished with encouragement to fresh efforts. But to this end an assignment must be compiled like a syllabus, indicating not only the ground to be covered, but containing helpful suggestions and lists of definite questions to be answered.

These helpful suggestions, or, as I prefer to call them, "interest pockets," should be a vital feature of the assignment. Here the teacher's knowledge of the psychology of each pupil comes into play. She must, in framing her assignment, take into consideration the special needs and

tastes of every child in her class. This is necessary in order to create "interest pockets." Instead of wording the assignments peremptorily
as, for example, "read such and such a reference,"
the pupil's interest will be aroused if it is
worded "you will find such and such references
helpful." Such phrasing catches the child's attention and thus these "interest pockets" give
life to the assignment. The assignments must not
tell too much but should stimulate research.

So constructed an assignment can almost be
made to serve as an assistant teacher. It is well
to indicate points where consultations with the
instructor is advisable, as, for instance, to a
mathematic assignment the words "After you
have finished the required problems come to me
and I will explain the next rule before you go on"
might be added. A pupil will appreciate any suggestion designed to facilitate his progress. We
must not do the work for him, but it is necessary
to provide inspiration for his efforts and occa-
sional help over a difficult bit of the road. The
ideal to be attained is to make him feel the interest
taken by the teacher in his progress without ren-
dering him dependent upon her. The introduction
of such "interest pockets" into assignments will
go a long ways towards the achievement of this
relationship.

But this relationship between teacher and pupil
should not be limited to one class or grade. It
is just as necessary that sympathy and interaction

should exist between the teachers as between the pupils in the school. Without it that inter-relation of subjects in the making up of the assignment cannot be achieved. In all schools a tendency exists on the part of each teacher to think his special subject of supreme importance in the curriculum. In her desire to do justice to it she is apt to encroach upon the time which ought to be devoted to other subjects. A satisfactory adjustment of all subjects in an assignment can only be made if all the teachers are ready to pool their collective knowledge of the psychology of the pupil, and their collective observation of the interests and capacity of each child. For this purpose the proposed assignments should be posted up for the benefit and discussion of the staff at least one week before they are exhibited on the notice boards to the pupils. In this way the teachers will be able to collaborate intelligently in adjusting and cutting down the amount of work set in each subject. Assignments thus become a problem to be shared and solved by the entire staff together.

For the welfare of the school as a whole it is essential that the complete scheme of work should be regarded as a synthesis. An examination of the assignment content will reveal how the work in each subject should be correlated. If, for example, a particularly interesting theme is assigned as a problem in science or in history, the English teacher should find in it good material for an essay, a debate, or for an oral conference. It is the province of the principal to emphasize that the importance given to the special subjects of each teacher in the assignment will depend upon a new presentation of that subject to the other instructors and upon the degree in which she secures their co-operation in its development.

This side of the assignment question is so vital that I will elaborate it by a concrete illustration. Take, for instance, the subject of art. The art department belongs to the whole school, not only to the art teacher, who simply assumes that responsibility for the whole staff. If art is merely work done in the studio, to be seen at the time of the annual exhibition, it is a dead thing. It can only be made a living influence if it permeates and serves every department. In order to do this the art teacher must secure the interest of her colleagues as well as of her pupils in the subject. To appeal to the latter to devote a large proportion of their time to any special subject on the grounds of its superior value is merely a waste of time. Better results will be attained if each instructor realizes that she must fit the subject into the general scheme, making it serve the needs of the whole, and getting her fellow teachers to ally their subjects with hers. Nor must it be forgotten that it is the teachers, not the pupils, who are responsible for changes made in the curriculum, and for the correlation of subjects in their assignments. The change in the attitude and appreciation of the pupils is the measure of their success.

The manner in which we have tackled the question in the Children's University School is worth quoting in this connection. There the geography teacher requires as a geography problem special notebooks which are made in the art laboratory. Note books are not the ultimate end of art, but the artistic note book is a means which elicits the appreciation of the geography teachers and extends the province of art. Supposing that the director of this department is working on an item of household decoration, she sends her pupils to the handwork room to do the necessary manual part of the job. When completed this manual work is brought back to the studio. The influence of such collaboration is valuable in unifying the aims of all the departments involved. But such correlation is only possible after an understanding has been reached between the heads of all departments. When the art instructor knows what work is assigned in geography and in other subjects, she can assign her problems in the art of the same period. She may begin through the medium of a notebook, but by making it beautiful the period becomes illuminated in the minds of the children, and so art gradually takes its place as a factor in their lives. Again, if the planetary system is under discussion in geography, the mathematics teacher can use it to illuminate problems in mathematics and algebra, while the art instructor calls attention to the beautiful celestial maps to be seen in the museums of the city. In principle there is beauty in every utilitarian thing. At the Children's University School the art and the music teachers have made their subjects so serve the needs of the others that art and music have penetrated as a living force into every laboratory. Consequently, art and music are recognized as equal in importance to every other subject studied, and an equal proportion of time is given to them. We have found that beauty vitalizes every study into which it is imported.

Each class or form adviser should, therefore, be furnished with copies of all the subject assignments used by her form, so that she may envisage the whole work concretely in advising each pupil on the best method of attacking his own allotment. With regard to those allotments it may not be found necessary in the case of older students, in university or in the last two years of a secondary school, to subdivide the monthly into weekly assignments. I suggest, however, that at the initiation of the Dalton Laboratory Plan it is advisable to give all pupils, regardless of age, the assistance of weekly divisions of work. Pupils who are accustomed to have all their work presented to them in the form of pre-digested oral lessons will find it very difficult at first to think in terms of the whole contract-job. The established habit of studying from day to day, living intellectually from hand to mouth cannot easily be discarded.

To concentrate instead on the organization of their work and the planning of their time demands an effort and perseverance in the effort. They will gradually learn to say themselves: "Where am I weak, and what must I do to perfect myself in this or that subject?" instead of "How much of this task must I do in order to escape reproof?" The change implies an entire change of attitude towards the work, and often towards the teacher. Pupils whose object is to do as little work as possible are extraordinarily quick in diagnosing the psychology of the different teachers. They know instinctively exactly what each teacher will exact and which are more easily satisfied. But thinking of the work in terms of Miss A or Miss B is, of course, fatal to the progress of the pupil in any direction. Morally speaking, it constitutes a grave danger, for it tempts the conscientious teacher to drive the pupil, and the more she sets herself to feed him with knowledge the less will he be inclined to assimilate it through his own effort. The more she teaches the less, in fact, will he learn.

In composing assignments, different subjects should of course be differently treated. Certain points should, however, always be emphasized irrespective of subject. If we want the pupil to dig and mine for himself we must give him the necessary tools for the operation. Teachers must guard against organizing their part of the ten or less different assignments in ten different ways, for the pupil cannot be expected to envisage his job as a whole unless all the parts are so correlated that it appears to him as really one problem. Lack of collaboration between the ten different teachers in the production of a consistent assignment scheme will be as deleterious to the child's mind and energy as if ten contractors were to work on a building without regard for the architect's design. Design is as essential to the construction of an assignment as it is to the construction of a house.

The following outline, which suggests types of things that ought to be included in an assignment, may prove useful, either in the case of monthly assignments with weekly subdivisions for young children, or without weekly subdivisions when the pupils are older and more advanced.

SUBJECT

(GRADE OR FORM)   (NO. OF CONTRACT ASSIGNMENT)

Points to be kept in mind

Preface to the Month's work.

1st Week

1. Topic
2. Problems
3. Written Work
4. Memory Work
5. Conferences or Oral Lessons
6. References

7. Equivalents (in days of work)
8. Bulletin Study
9. Departmental Cuts.

For the second, third, and fourth weeks some or all of these points may be included. In any case all should be kept in mind, for each subdivision must be a definite unit in itself as well as a part of the whole month's assignment. A settled procedure with, as far as possible, uniformity of headings, etc., is desirable. The number of the contract assignments is, or course, determined by the number of months in the school year; for example:

FORM	SUBJECT	CONTRACT ASSIGNMENT
II	Geography	3

These points will bear some elaboration for the benefit of inexperienced teachers.

Preface. This should be a simple statement consisting of a few sentences designed to introduce the assignment of work. Above all, the preface should be an "interest pocket."

Topic. By this term I mean phases or aspects of a general subject. Supposing the subject to be geography, the topic might be "China," "Petroleum," or "The Peace Conference." To young children a topic should always be given. It will furnish a central idea to be developed.

Problems. This word includes a variety of things. We can set problems in the form of maps to be drawn; measurements to be approximated; routes to be traced; or pictures to be studied when a definite object is to be accomplished or a particular reaction is to be stimulated. Problems may also include examples or theorems to be worked out; translations; transpositions or themes in music; a stencilled design or a block-print in art; experiments in science; or a set drill when given to fix a point or to illustrate a rule.

Written Work. Under this heading all the written work required should be listed with dates when it is to be handed in. This applies to work written either in notebooks or otherwise.

Memory Work. This heading covers poetry to be learnt by heart; rules or tables; verbs or songs; theorems, treaties, preambles, etc.

Conferences. Here the date on which particular subjects are to be discussed at the oral lesson should be indicated so that the pupils may prepare for such discussions on their own responsibility and have their exhibits, etc., ready.

References. Under this heading the names and, if the assignment is long, the pages of all reference books or magazine articles should be given with directions showing where such books are to be found.

Equivalents. Here it is essential to show a pupil how to record his progress on his own contract graph, for it is a picture of his accomplishment and a compass which enables him to discover and satisfy his needs. His graph should be taken from laboratory to laboratory and to all class conferences. It is his ticket of admission and should be accurately marked, daily as he goes on. It is the psychological picture of his job. Except on rare occasions he does not do all the month's or even all the week's work at a sitting. Thus, if in any one week's assignment grammar, translation, and oral work are required, say, in a foreign language, a time equivalent should be stated. Grammar, for instance, might count as two days' or units of work, translation as two days' work, and oral reading as one day's work. In a monthly assignment, when the subject is English, his review of the book in question might count as—reading, one week's work, and the written part as three weeks' work.

Bulletin Study. This point should be marked whenever the laboratory bulletin board displays maps or pictures which are to be studied in connection with a special phase of any subject, or when pupils are expected to add to the collection displayed.

Departmental Cuts. As I have already dealt with this matter it suffices to repeat here that work requirements are departmentally cut when credit is given for work done in any subject as if it were done in another correlated subject. If, for instance, a paper in science is written in sufficiently good English to be accepted as work done in English composition, the amount of the contract-job is departmentally cut down in proportion. Whenever work is credited it should always be stated as such in the assignment.

The headings of Problems, Written Work, and Memory Work represent points which are very closely related. The problem may sometimes actually be memory work, while at other times the memory work may be supplementary to the real problem. In English a written book review may be the problem set, whereas in science the problem set may be an experiment of which the written description is supplementary. If the written work is required, not as a problem but to record a problem, this should be stated under the heading of "Written Work."

But the main and most important point to keep in mind in composing an assignment is that it must clearly demonstrate to the pupil what his job really is. He must be told distinctly what is expected of him, and the difficulties he is likely to meet in the execution of it must be indicated. I hope the training schools of the future may prepare expert specialists to whom all this will be plain. To succeed in producing really valuable instructors for our schools, consideration must be given to the cultural background and the cultural needs of the teachers. Sufficient training in psychology to enable teachers to understand the child's nature, its mental processes and their development, should also be a vital part of their equipment. In the case of specialists, facilities for intensive training covering the entire field in one subject must also be provided.

To the teacher who appreciates the character and the needs of girls and boys, and who makes of the human material in her charge her primary study, the reorganization of school life on the Dalton Laboratory Plan will present no difficulty. Nor if she knows her subject thoroughly will she be inclined to limit it to purely local aspects. In the United States to-day history is taught far too generally from the mere national point of view. Frequently pupils are given an unconscious impression that "the world began" in the American year 1776! This may be considered patriotic by some, but the narrowing influence of such teaching upon the pupil is evident. Only by learning history as world history, and all subjects on the basis of the universe, can the child grow into a complete man or woman as well as a good citizen.

CHAPTER VI

SAMPLE ASSIGNMENTS

ON the principle that example is better than precept I am devoting this chapter to a collection of sample assignments. In order to illustrate the application of the points to be kept in mind in their composition I begin by quoting two examples of one Science Assignment for eighth grade pupils. The first is, I consider, inadequate because it fails to give sufficient detail or direction to the child in the execution of his job. In the second example as you will see this fault is corrected. Its preface contains the necessary "interest pocket," the true equivalents are clearly stated; the whole is calculated so as to provide a perspective of the entire contract and to stimulate interaction and discussion among the voluntary class-groups in the laboratory.

I may call attention here to the fact that assignments are not split up into definite daily requirements. To do so would rob the pupil of interest and of the necessary freedom in organizing his time according to the needs of his work.

ASSIGNMENT A

(Inadequate Version)

Grade VIII SCIENCE *5th Contract Assignment*

1st Week

MOTION AND FORCE.

First, I want you to learn Sir Isaac Newton's Three Laws of Motion. These you will find in Section I, Chapter III, in Higgins. Study this section very carefully, do the experiment on page 47, find out all you can about Sir Isaac Newton in an encyclopedia, and then write the answers to the questions on page 49 in your notebooks. (Three days' work.)

In continuing your work you will find out some of the effects of Newton's Laws. Read what is said about this in Higgins, pp. 50-54, as far as paragraph 64. There are six experiments to be done, and be sure that you know what is meant by inertia, momentum, centre of gravity, base and equilibrium. (Two days' work.)

2nd Week

This week we shall continue to study the effects of Newton's Laws. Study Higgins, pp. 54-60. There are seven experiments to do, and I want you to write the results of these in your notebooks. (Two days' work.)

Write the answers to the questions on pp. 59-60. (Two days' work.)

WORK AND MACHINES.

Study very carefully pp. 60-66 in Higgins. (One day's work.)

3rd Week

WORK AND MACHINES (*continued*).

Turn to p. 173 in Caldwell and Eikenberry and think over the answers to the questions, and then come and discuss them with me. (One day's work.)

On p. 176 in C. and E. there are six illustrations showing different types of levers. Write in your notebook which class of levers each one of these articles illustrates. (One day's work.)

In Cummings, Nature Study, on ll. 231-232-233 there are some experiments with pulleys that I want you to do. All the questions are to be written in your notebook. (Experiments equal one day's work and the questions count as two days' work.)

4th Week

WORK AND MACHINES (*continued*).

With a series of four pulleys I want you to arrange the most efficient combination you can for raising a heavy weight. (One day's work.)

Read Chapter XV in C. and E. (Two days' work.)

Answer the questions of p. 66 in Higgins (to be written: one day's work).

With the meccano set construct a model of a machine such as a Travelling Jib Crane—24, p. 10 in Manual of Instructions.

ASSIGNMENT A

(Amended Version)

Grade VIII SCIENCE *5th Contract Assignment*

1st **Week**

MOTION AND FORCE.

1. Will an automobile start without an explosion of the gasoline? What makes a screw go into wood? Why do we oil our bicycles? Why do we use pulleys? Have you never wondered about these things? Daily we notice things that happen all about us, but seldom do we stop to consider *how* they happen!

This month we are going to learn something about these common everyday happenings which are explained by certain fundamental laws in physics. We are going to consider some of the common types of machines and discover how they are able to accomplish the work that they do. In order to have a good understanding of machines it is important that we know something about motion and force. Therefore, in starting our work for the month we shall consider motion and force first.

NEWTON'S THREE LAWS OF MOTION AND THEIR EFFECTS.

You will find it helpful to learn these three laws first and then proceed with the following experiments. (See reference No. 1.)

EXPERIMENT 1. A CHANGE OF MOTION FOLLOWS THE
DIRECTION OF THE FORCE WHICH CAUSES IT, AND
IS PROPORTIONAL TO THE AMOUNT OF FORCE USED
AND THE TIME DURING WHICH IT ACTS.

Directions. Suspend a small ball on a long
string. Snap it at the same instant with one
finger of each hand in directions that are at
right angles to each other. Observe the direction
in which the ball moves.

Before undertaking the following experiments
which have to do with the effects of Newton's
Laws it is necessary to have some understanding
of these effects. (See reference 2, and then verify
your reading with the following experiments.)

EXPERIMENT 2. INERTIA.

Directions. Balance a visiting card on the end
of your finger and place a coin upon it directly
above the finger tip. With the other hand suddenly snap the card away edgewise. Why doesn't
the coin move off with the card?

EXPERIMENT 3. MOMENTUM.

Directions. Using the same ball, roll it twice
over the same surface, once slowly and once with
speed. Note the distance that it travels.

Now take two balls, one much heavier than the
other, roll them over the surface, starting them
at the same speed. Note the distances travelled.

EXPERIMENT 4. CENTRE OF GRAVITY.

Directions. Try to balance a ruler on your
finger. Where is the centre of mass of the ruler?

Compare the quantity of matter on both sides of this point. How do you think the action of gravity upon one side of this spot compares with that upon the other? Where is the centre of gravity of the ruler? Now hang unequal weights on the ruler and find the centre of gravity of the whole.

Find the centre of gravity on your ruler by balancing and mark the point. Now place the ruler on a table, push it over the edge little by little, and note the position of its centre of gravity just before it falls.

WRITTEN WORK

Questions. (See references 1 and 2.)

1. State Newton's three laws of motion. Tell all that you know about Newton. (See reference 3.)

2. Give any examples of bodies that seem to set themselves in motion, and tell what outside force moves them. Why do we not find on earth any examples of constant motion without force being applied?

3. If two equal forces act upon a body in opposite directions, what would be the result? If the forces were unequal what would be the result?

4. What is meant by reaction? Could there be any reaction if there were no action? Is there ever any action without reaction?

5. Give examples of reaction. Explain some of its uses. Show how a screw propeller moves a boat.

6. If you strike a wall with your fist you feel

pain. Why does it not give equal pain if you strike a pillow with your fist?

References

1. Higgins—First Science Book, Chapter III, Section 1.
2. Higgins—First Science Book, pp. 50-54.
3. To find out about Sir Isaac Newton see the American Educator or some encyclopedia. Some of you may also be interested in consulting our new magazine editions of The Outlines of Science by Prof. J. Arthur Thomson. These have just arrived from England.

Equivalents

Experiments will count as two days' work; written work will count as one day's work; references will count as two days' work.

2nd Week

SOME MORE EFFECTS OF NEWTON'S LAWS.

Our business for this week has to do with other effects of Newton's Laws. You will consider these in the following order: Stability, Centrifugal Force, Law of Falling Bodies, and the Pendulum. Before doing the experiments which will make these things clear to you it will be helpful to consult the reference.

EXPERIMENT 1. STABILITY.

Directions. Stand your pencil on its end; then lay it on its side. In which position has it the broader base? In which is it the more stable?

Pile up three books and test the stability of the pile. Then add as many more books as you can, and test that. Which pile is the more stable? Why?

Try to balance your ruler, first on its side and then on its end. Which is easier, and why?

Experiment 2. Centrifugal Force.

Directions. Tie a string to a small wooden ball and swing it rapidly about the hand in a circle. Do you have to use force to hold it? Why? Suddenly let the ball go free and note its motion. What direction does it tend to take? Try the same thing with a very short string and a very long one, and explain the difference. Note that the two forces exactly balance each other; for while one acts toward and the other away from the centre, the ball moves no nearer and no farther from the centre than the length of the string allows. As soon as you let go both forces cease to act and the ball obeys the first law of motion.

Experiment 3. Falling Bodies.

Directions. Drop two balls of exactly the same size, one of wood and the other of lead, exactly together from the same height, and note carefully whether they strike together or not. Repeat this several times to be sure that the results that you obtain are accurate.

Compare these with the fall of a sheet of paper.

Experiment 4. The Pendulum.

Directions. Make two pendulums of the same length, using a wooden ball and a lead ball. Start them swinging exactly together and compare the rates of their vibrations, that is, the number of swings made by each in a certain period of time. What effect has the weight of the ball upon the vibration rate of the pendulum?

Swing a pendulum through a small arc and count its vibrations for 15 seconds. Now swing the same pendulum through a much greater arc and count its vibrations for 15 seconds. What effect has the length of the arc upon the rate of vibration? (The length of the arc makes a slight difference in rate if one arc is much greater than the other, and none at all if both arcs are small.)

Make a pendulum 4 inches long, and another 16 inches long, and compare their rates of vibration. How much longer is the second than the first? Which vibrates the faster? What thing do you find to make a marked difference in the vibration rate of the pendulum?

Written Work

Questions.

1. What is inertia? State examples. Why can you not start a bicycle at once at your greatest speed?

2. What is momentum? Upon what two factors does it depend? How is it generally measured?

3. A rifle ball weighing half an ounce moves at the rate of one thousand feet a second, while a forty-pound cannon ball moves at a rate of one foot per second. Which has the greater momentum?

4. Why does a woodcutter sometimes fasten his axe in a stick and then invert it, striking the block with the stick uppermost?

5. Why can you not stand an egg on its end? If there were a hole straight through the earth's centre from surface to surface, how far into it would a falling body go?

6. Under what conditions will a body be supported from falling?

7. Upon what does the stability of a body depend, and how? Why is it hard to walk upon stilts?

8. Explain the cause of centrifugal force. State examples of it. Why do you lean in turning a corner? Why is the inside rail of a track placed lower?

9. How far will a body fall in one second? In two seconds? Why does a body constantly increase its speed as it falls? Why is more damage done by a longer fall as a rule?

10. Describe a pendulum. What force causes it to swing downward? Why does it then swing upward? If no force but gravity opposed its upward swing, how far would it go as compared with its downward swing?

References

Millikan and Gale—Practical Physics, pp. 81-87.

Equivalents

The reference will count as one day's work. The experiments will count as two days' work. The written work will count as two days' work.

3rd Week

WORK AND MACHINES.

What is work? What is gained by using levers, pulleys, wedges, inclined planes, etc.? These things are all simple machines, and our task for this week is to discover the answers to these questions. Before going on with the experiments you will find it helpful to consult the first reference.

EXPERIMENT 1. PULLEYS.

Fasten a pulley to some convenient support, and pass over it a cord having a given weight fastened to one end of it, and a spring balance to the other. Compare the weight with the force measured by the spring balance in raising it.

EXPERIMENT 2. PULLEYS.

Attach a weight to a movable pulley and note the amount of power required to sustain it.

EXPERIMENT 3. PULLEYS.

Arrange one fixed and two movable pulleys supporting a weight, and note the amount of power required to sustain it. What advantage is gained by the use of the fixed pulley? What part of the weight does each section of the string support?

Written Work

Questions.

1. In the case of one movable pulley what part of the weight is supported by the spring balance? By the hook?

2. In the case of one movable pulley in what

direction does the power act, and how could this direction be changed by using a fixed pulley?

3. When one movable pulley is used through, how much space must the power pass in raising the weight one foot? When one fixed pulley is used?

4. When you have one fixed and two movable pulleys what portion of the weight is supported by the fixed pulley? By the balance?

5. In the case of 4, how far must the power move to raise the weight one foot? What is gained by using two movable pulleys? What is lost? How do the loss and gain compare?

6. If another fixed pulley were added in the case of 4, what would be the effect? If another movable pulley were added, what would be the effect?

7. Upon what does the power gained in using a block and tackle depend? State a rule for computing it.

References

Higgins—First Science Book, pp. 60-66.

Equivalents

The references will count as one day's work each (two days); the experiments will count as one day's work; the written work will count as two days' work.

4th Week

WORK AND MACHINES—*continued*.

PROBLEM. I think that now you will find it interesting to see the application of some of the machines and principles in a machine of your own. Accordingly, I want you to construct a model of a Travelling Jib Crane, with the Meccano set. In operating it you will notice how the lever and pulleys are combined to good advantage.

Written Work

Questions.

1. What is work, how is it measured, and what is the unit of work?

2. What is meant by power? What is the unit of the rate of doing work? How much is one foot pound?

3. What is a machine? Can a machine do work of itself?

4. What in general is the use of machines to man?

5. State the law of machines and show how a lever applies this law.

6. Why do tailor's shears have long blades and short handles, while plumber's shears have short blades and long handles?

7. Why does a bicycle of high gear run harder than one of low gear?

8. State the advantage given by a lever of the second class; of the third class.

9. Name some familiar uses of the screw.

10. Explain the use of gear wheels in machinery.

Conference

You will report to me for a conference after you have read the following reference on "Some Common Types of Work."

References

Caldwell and Eikenberry—General Science, Chapter XV.

Equivalents

The problem will count as two days' work; the written work will count as one day's work; the conference will count as one day's work; the reference will count as one day's work.

HISTORY ASSIGNMENTS

Assignment No. 1

(For Fourth Grade Pupils of 8 to 9 years.)

Grade IV HISTORY *5th Contract Assignment*

After Paul Revere had warned the "Minute Men" that the British were coming, and after the British had been beaten back from Concord there was no fighting for some months. The British were perfectly satisfied to stay in Boston and not meddle with the "Minute Men." On June 17th, 1775, the British saw that the "Minute Men" had put up a fort on Bunker Hill in Charlestown. If the British did not drive the Americans off the hill, the Americans might drive the British out of Boston. The British attacked Bunker Hill, and after being driven back twice with great loss of life, they finally succeeded in driving the Americans away, because the Americans had used up all their ammunition. In the summer General George Washington came to take command of the American army near Boston, and in the spring of the next year, by mounting some cannon on Dorchester Heights, near Boston, he made the British get into their ships and sail away. Washington then went to New York, and the British came there also soon after. This time the British were successful, and Washington was driven out of New York and across New Jersey, with the British in hot pursuit. When Washington crossed the Delaware River into Pennsylvania, the British gave up the chase, thinking they had frightened him away for good and all.

1st Week

This week we are going to read how Washington surprised the British when they least expected it. There will be two problems to work on.

Problems

PROBLEM 1. Suppose you are one of Washington's soldiers at the time the British were chasing him across New Jersey and into Pennsylvania. Write the story of how you crossed the Delaware River with Washington on Christmas night, and how you took Trenton.

PROBLEM 2. Again supposing you are one of Washington's men. This time you are with the American army at Valley Forge during the winter of 1776-77, when the British were snugly housed in Philadelphia, and when Washington, with his poor little army, was shivering at Valley Forge. Write a letter home to your children telling them of your life in camp.

References

The reference for these problems is *American Hero Stories*. Use the index to find the stories you want. One is called "A Christmas Surprise" and the other "Winter at Valley Forge."

Equivalents

Each of these problems counts as two-and-a-half days' work. Bring your compositions to me when you have finished them.

Departmental Cut

This written work, when accepted by me, may be credited as a week's work in English Composition.

2nd Week

In the summer of 1776 a very important thing happened in Philadelphia. It was before the British captured the city, and it was not a battle. The Declaration of Independence was signed on July 4th. That is what we shall study about this week. I presume you know something about it already. Perhaps you can find out some more about it.

Problems

Here are some questions on the Declaration of Independence. Write the answers to them, using complete sentences in each answer.

1. Who were in the Continental Congress?
2. Where did it meet, and when?

3. What two important deeds did the Continental Congress do?

4. Who introduced the resolution for Independence?

5. What five men were on the committee?

6. Who wrote the Declaration of Independence?

7. How was the news of the Declaration of Independence told to the people?

8. What was the exact date of the Declaration of Independence?

Memory Work

Learn by heart the last paragraph of the Declaration, beginning: "We, therefore, the Representatives of the United States of America——"

References

The reference for this work is *Makers of the Nation.*

Bulletin Study and Conference

Will you all examine the copy of the Declaration of Independence that is on the Bulletin Board? At the Conference on Friday, February 17th, we shall talk about the Declaration, and I shall ask you what you have noticed about this copy of the Declaration.

Equivalents

The reading counts as one day's work; the questions as two days' work; and the memory work as two days' work.

3rd Week

This week we shall read and study about one of the martyrs of the Revolution. I wonder if you all know what a martyr is. If you do not know, see if you can find out. This martyr's name was Nathan Hale.

Problem

Your problem this week will be to read about Nathan Hale, and then to come to me and let me test you on your reading. I am giving you some questions here to guide you as you study about him.

1. Where was Nathan Hale born?
2. Where did he go to College?
3. Tell about his offering to go on the dangerous mission for Washington.
4. What was his disguise?
5. Tell about his adventures and about his capture.
6. What was done to him?
7. What were his last words?

Equivalents

The reading will count as two days' work, and the reporting on the reading as three days' work.

4th Week

There are a great many heroes of the Revolutionary War that we might read about. We have not time to read about all of them, but I am hoping that you may be interested to find out more about some of them. Here are some of the interesting ones: Ethan Allen, Benedict Arnold, Colonel Prescott, General Gates, General Herkimer, Israel Putnam, Mad Anthony Wayne, Daniel Morgan, The Swamp Will o' the Wisp, Nathaniel Greene, Lafayette, Baron Von Steuben, Robert Morris, George Rogers Clark.

This week we shall learn about one more great Revolutionary hero, John Paul Jones, the "Father of the American Navy."

Problem

The problem is to read about John Paul Jones and then to come to me and give me an oral report on your reading. I shall expect you to come and tell me what you have to say without any questioning or help on my part. Plan your report out before you come to me.

I shall ask some of the children who give good reports to repeat them at the conference on February 24th.

References

The references for this work are *American Hero Stories* or *Makers of the Nation.*

Equivalents

The reading counts as two days' work, and the report as three days' work.

Assignment No. 2

(For Fifth Grade Pupils 9 to 10 years.)

Grade V   HISTORY   *5th Contract Assignment*

The Persian Wars had ended, and the Greeks were no longer afraid of attacks by the Persians.

The Athenians went home to find their homes in ruins, for you will remember that the Persians had burned Athens just before the battle of Salamis. The Spartans went home planning to make their city the greatest in Greece. In fact, each city had great plans of this same kind. Although they had all united for the time being to drive out the Persians, each city was jealous of its neighbours, and we shall see what hard times the Greeks had in the next three hundred years.

1st Week

This week we shall study one of the great Athenian heroes, Pericles. He is, perhaps, the greatest of all the great Athenian leaders.

Problem

After you have done the reading listed below, write out the answers to the following questions, using complete sentences in every answer:

1. Tell the story of the Athenians rebuilding their walls.
2. What was Piraeus?
3. Describe the Long Walls.
4. What are the names of the three kinds of columns used in Greek temples?
5. What were the names of two buildings on the Acropolis?
6. Tell what each building was used for.
7. Describe the Theatre of Dionysius.
8. Who were the three great Greek tragic writers?
9. What is a tragedy? What is a comedy?

10. Who was a comedy writer in Athens?
11. Who were two historians?
12. What changes did Pericles make in the laws of Athens?

References

Read in *Old World Hero Stories* the story called "Pericles."

Equivalents

The reading counts as two days' work, and the writing as three days' work.

2nd Week

We shall learn more about the Age of Pericles this week.

Problems

There will be three problems this week.

1. Draw a plan of the front of the Parthenon, naming the different parts.

2. Write a description of a Greek house. Tell how the house was arranged, and compare it with a modern house.

3. Tell, in a story, what the children in Athens did. Tell how they were taught, how they played, etc.

References

The reference for 1 is Tarbell's *History of Greek Art*. The reference for 2 and 3 is *Old World Hero Stories*.

Equivalents

Problem 1 will count for three days' work and 2 and 3 each one day.

Bulletin Study

Examine the pictures of the Parthenon and of Greek houses that are on the Bulletin Board. These may help you in your work.

Departmental Cut

Miss Baily is willing to credit you with three days' work in Art for the drawing of the Parthenon.

3rd Week

After the time of Pericles the Athenians had a hard time. They had a war with the Spartans, and the Spartans won. The Athenians were never again as happy and as prosperous as they were when Pericles was their leader. Almost three hundred years later there arose a great kingdom to the north of Greece, called Macedonia. The king of this realm was named Philip, and he had a son named Alexander. This is the man we are going to study this week.

Problems

PROBLEM 1. Here are some questions to answer about Alexander. Write the answers in complete sentences.

1. What tidings did the three messengers bring to King Philip of Macedonia?

2.   Tell the story of the taming of Bucephalus.

3.   Who was Alexander's teacher, and where did he come from?

4.   After Philip's death what did Alexander decide to do?

5.   How big an army did he have?

6.   What were three of his battles?

7.   Tell the story of the Gordian Knot.

8.   How many cities were named after Alexander?

PROBLEM 2.   The second problem is to draw a map of Alexander's kingdom.   Use coloured crayons to show the territory that he conquered.

References

Read about Alexander in *Old World Hero Stories,* and find the map of his empire in West's *Ancient World.*

Equivalents

The reading is one day's work; the writing is two days' work; and the drawing is two days' work.

4th Week

This week we are going to start on the study of Rome.   The first topic is the Founding of the City.

Problems

There will be two parts to the work this week. PROBLEM 1.   First we shall all read the story of Romulus, and be prepared to make an oral report on it.

Problem 2. I shall assign different stories to certain members of our group, and those certain members will be responsible for telling that story at the conference on December 19th. These small groups may work together and plan about the telling of their stories in any way they wish. Here are the stories:

The Story of Aeneas
        Margery, Edward, Harry, Jane, Mary.

The Stealing of the Sabine women
        Doris, Louise, Donald, John.

The Women stop the Fight
        Richard, Helen B., Joseph.

The Treachery of Tarpeia
        Edith, Alice, Eleanor, Arthur, Horace.

References

The references for these stories are: *Old World Hero Stories, The Story of the Romans, The Story of the Roman People.*

Equivalents

Problems 1 and 2 count as half a week's work each.

Bulletin Study

You will all be interested in looking at the pictures on the Bulletin Board illustrating the Story of Aeneas and the Founding of Rome.

(For Sixth Grade Pupils 10 to 11 years.)

Grade VI   *5th ContractAssignment*
ENGLISH HISTORY

Edward III, the King of England who started
the Hundred Years' War with France, had six
sons. We have already read about the Black
Prince; he died before he could become king, and
not one of Edward's other sons became kings
either. Some of their descendants, however, did
ascend the throne, the first one being Richard II,
about whom we have read. Then came Henry IV,
the son of the Duke of Lancaster. Henry V was
another Lancastrian, and his son Henry VI, was
also a Lancastrian. Henry VI was a very young
boy, and many people thought that the crown
should go to another descendant of Edward III,
the Duke of York. This led to disputes, and the
disputes to more violent forms of argument, until
there was started in England a war known as the
Wars of the Roses. This was called so because
the Lancastrians took for their emblem a red rose
and the Yorkists, as the followers of the Duke of
York were called, took a white rose for their
emblem.

1st Week

We shall study about the Wars of the Roses this
week.

Problem

The problem is to read as much as you can
about these wars, and then come to me for an oral

test on what you have read. I suggest that as you read you write down on paper the things that you think are important, and that you want to remember.

References

The references are in *Piers Plowman, Bk. VI, The Story of the English,* or *England's Story.*

Equivalents

The reading will count as 3 days' work; the oral test as 2 days.

2nd Week

We shall study some particular incidents in the Wars of the Roses this week.

Problem

The problem will be to write a composition on one of the following topics:—
1. Queen Margaret and the Robber.
2. The Princes in the Tower.
3. The First English Printer.

References

The references are the same as last week.
NOTE: In writing this composition, remember to put in all marks of punctuation, all capitals, etc.

Departmental Cut

If this composition passes it may count as a week's work in your English composition.

3rd Week

Problem

You are a reporter on an English newspaper.
(We will pretend that they had newspapers in the
time of Richard III.) You have been assigned to
write up the Battle of Bosworth Field. Tell how
the battle came to be fought, tell about the battle
itself, and tell what came of it. Get your material
from any of the English History Books. Here is
a head-line for your story.
"Crowned on the Battlefield."

4th Week

The family of English kings that began with
Henry VII was called the Tudor family. There
were five of them, Henry VII, Henry VIII,
Edward VI, Mary and Elizabeth. I wish we had
time to read about them all and about some of the
great men who lived in their time. We shall have
to pass over them, or most of them, and come to
the reign of Elizabeth, perhaps the greatest of the
Tudors.

Problem

We shall have two problems this week, and each
one will be the subject of an oral report. I will
give you the problems, and I am going to let you
find your material for yourselves. You are
familiar enough by this time with the various
books we have and can easily find your own reading.

PROBLEM 1. The Spanish Armada; what it was;

why it came to England; how the English made ready to meet it; the storm; the battle; the end of the Armada.

PROBLEM 2. The Elizabethan Age; what is meant by that name; what the names of the great figures of that age are; what they did.

Equivalents

Each problem and its oral report will count as one-half a week's work.

ASSIGNMENT No. 4

(For Seventh Grade Pupils 11 to 12 years)

Grade VII　　　　　　*5th Contract Assignment*
AMERICAN HISTORY

One Month's Assignment

After the delegates at the Philadelphia Convention had made the Constitution, and the nine states had agreed to it, thus making it a law, the country was ready to start governing itself. As soon as possible the people met to elect a President, and they all united in choosing George Washington for the first one. We have had twenty-eight since Washington. From now on we are going to study our history in a little different way, that is, studying what went on during the administration of each president. We shall keep a note-book, which I will give you, and record the things we find out about the different presidents. We shall have at least a page for each president, and for some we shall have to have more than one page, when there were a great many important happenings.

Problem

Our problem this month will be the preparing in our note-books of the material about eleven of the presidents, beginning with Washington and ending with James K. Polk.

In your note-books put the name of the president on the top line of the page. After his name in parentheses put the name of the political party that he belonged to and the dates of his administration. On the line below put the name of the vice-president, or vice-presidents if he had two. Then skip a line and begin to put down the important facts to remember about that president's administration. Number the facts, and begin each on a new line. It would be a good plan to put the facts down on paper first, and show them to me, and then copy them into your book. Be sure to consult me if you have any doubt about the work. Here is a sample arrangement of a page:

George Washington (Federalist) 1789-1797.

John Adams, Vice-President.

1. Inaugurated in New York, April 30, 1789.
2. ————
3. ————

References

To get the material for your note-book read Montgomery's *Elementary History,* or Montgomery's *Leading Facts.* Use the *World Almanac* for information about the vice-presidents.

Equivalents

You can figure out how much to mark on your card as you work. There are eleven presidents, and there are twenty working days. Therefore some presidents would count as two days' work, but some as only one.

Assignment No. 5

(For Eighth Grade Pupils 12 to 13 years.)

AMERICAN HISTORY

Grade VIII   CIVICS *5th Contract Assignment*

Last month you studied about the Constitution of the United States: you learned about the legislative, executive, and judicial departments, and what their different powers and duties were. This month we shall review this by comparing these same departments with those in another country; we shall learn about some of the great figures in public life of to-day; and we shall go and find out some more necessary and useful knowledge about our Constitution.

1st Week

We are all interested in England, because the people there speak the same language that we do, and because our forefathers came from that country. This week we are going to see how the parts of the Government of England are different from the parts of our own, and how they are alike.

Problem

The problem will be to learn these likenesses and differences so that you can explain them to anyone in a clear way. I shall test you on what you have learned, either orally or by written test.

References

In a pamphlet called Pupils' Outlines for Home Study, Civics, Part I, pages 10-14, you will find the necessary facts about the Governments of the United States and England given in parallel columns.

Equivalents

You will probably wish to do the whole week's work at one time, but if you do not do it all at once, consult me as to the value of portions of the work outline.

2nd Week

In connection with the studying we did last week, we are going to learn some current events this week; we are going to find out who some of the men are who are holding the various positions in the Governments we have been studying. You may know some of them without looking them up.

1. President of the United States.
2. King of England.
3. Vice-President of the United States.
4. Prince of Wales.
5. Members of the Cabinet of the United States.
6. Members of the English Cabinet.

7. United States Ambassador to England.
8. English Ambassador to the United States.
9. United States Ambassador to France.
10. United States Ambassador to Italy.
11. United States Ambassador to Belgium.
12. Judges of the United States Supreme Court.
13. The Senators from New York State.
14. Speaker of the House of Representatives.
15. Governor of the Philippines.
16. United States Delegates to the Disarmament Conference.

References

You can find this information in *The World Almanac*, 1922.

Bulletin Study

There are pictures of some of the men in this assignment on the Bulletin board. See if you can add to the collection from pictures in the current magazines or the picture supplements of the Sunday papers.

3rd Week

Before we leave the study of the government of the United States there are a few things we ought to know as intelligent citizens. We shall learn some of those things this week.

Problems

PROBLEM 1. How a Law is passed through Congress.
PROBLEM 2. How the Constitution is amended. What is an amendment?

PROBLEM 3. The amendments: what they contain; learn Nos. I-XVIII.

When you have finished the study of these problems, come to me and make me an oral report on what you have found.

References

By this time you are sufficiently familiar with the various books on government that we have, to have some general idea as to where to find things, so I am going to leave you to use your own ingenuity in digging out information that you want.

Equivalents

The first two problems count as 2 days' work; the last as 3 days'.

4th Week

This week we have three more problems in the same line as last week's. The first two are to be written out, and the last one I will test you on when you have finished.

Problems

PROBLEM 1. What does the Constitution prohibit the States from doing?

PROBLEM 2. What rights do the States have?

PROBLEM 3. Learn the following definitions. (Any person who wants to talk intelligently about affairs of government should know what these terms mean.)

1. Congress—A body of men who make the

laws for the United States, this body consists of the House of Representatives and the Senate.

2. Legislative Department—Department that has to do with the making of laws.

3. Executive Department—Department that sees that the laws are carried out.

4. Judicial Department—Department that explains the laws and sentences law-breakers.

5. Original jurisdiction—A court is said to have original jurisdiction if a case is begun in that court.

6. Appellate jurisdiction—A court is said to have appellate jurisdiction if a case is brought to it from a lower court.

7. Admiralty—Jurisdiction of cases arising from maritime affairs and crimes committed on the high seas.

8. Ambassador—an official representing his country in a foreign country.

9. Consul—An official representing his country in a foreign country mainly for the protection of commerce.

10. Impeachment—accusing a public officer of crime or misbehaviour while in office.

11. Habeas Corpus—A warrant compelling the investigation as to the legality of the imprisonment of an individual.

12. Ex Post Facto Law—Makes an act criminal which was not so when committed.

References

The material for the first two problems may be found in the Constitution itself or in one of the books on government.

Equivalents

The first problem counts as 2 days' work; the second as 1 day's and the third as 2 days'.

GEOGRAPHY ASSIGNMENTS

ASSIGNMENT No. 1

(For Eighth Grade Pupils of 12 to 13 years.)

Grade VIII   *4th Contract Assignment*
GEOGRAPHY

TOPIC: CHINA.

You already know about some of China's problems through your study of the Conference for the Limitation of Armaments. I think you will be interested in learning more about this extraordinary nation of 400,000,000 people, whose natural abilities seem not less than ours, although their manners and customs are so very different.

The civilization of China is probably 2,000 years older than that of Europe—that is to say, about 4,000 years old. Some say it is much older.

1st Week

Problems

PROBLEM 1. The three great Chinese religions are all much older than that of Christ. The founder of Buddhism was a native of India. Confucius and Lao-Tsin were Chinamen who gave their names to great religions. You will read about them all in Van Loon's story of Mankind, pp. 240-250.   Write about half a page on each religion.

PROBLEM 2.   Study carefully both the map on p. 243 and the illustration on p. 249.

PROBLEM 3.   You will find on the shelves a set of pictures of Chinese life which will repay careful study.   Each picture is explained by a little paragraph which should always be read in connection with it.   There are many pictures of Chinese life in the back numbers of *Asia* and the *Geographic*. I will put some of these magazines aside for you.

PROBLEM 4.   Write a page about your first impressions as a traveller in China.   Write as you feel, about the things that interest you.

Mr. Klauber has spent some time in China.   He will speak in assembly on Thursday, and will bring some interesting pictures, coins, and paper money as a loan exhibit for the museum.

Equivalents

Problem 1 will count as one-and-a-half days' work; problem 2 as half a day's; problem 3 as one day's; problem 4 as one day's.

Departmental Cut

Consult the head of the English Department to see how much these papers will count for English. After they are corrected and satisfactory, re-copy them in your notebook on religions.

2nd Week

There is a good map of China and the Far East on p. 17 of your exercise book.   You will find it much simpler and clearer than the map of the Pacific.

Problems

PROBLEM 1.   Name water bodies, land bodies, peninsulas, countries, provinces, rivers, and canals as directed in Exs. XIX and XX.

PROBLEM 2.   Read pp. 200-235 in Asia, a geography reader.   In your notes lay special stress on the causes of China's age-long isolation, the density of the population, and the poverty of the working-class.

In case several people should want to do this work at the same time, I can assign reading in other books.

NOTE: Two Chinese students will be with us in your Geography Conference on Thursday.   They will give suggestions for costuming the Chinese play *Mulan,* and answer any questions you may ask.

Equivalents

Problem 1 will count as two days' work; problem 2 as three days' work.

3rd Week

Problems

PROBLEM 1.   Read about the Chinese Republic in Robinson's *Commercial* or Dodge's *Advanced Geography.*   Take notes and answer these questions:

1.   Why is the population of China crowded into certain provinces?   Give details.

2. Why do the Chinese object to labour-saving machinery?

3. Can you explain why they have progressed so little in 2,000 years?

PROBLEM 2. Find out how silk is produced and write about it. Refer to American Educator, or advertising material on shelves. Find out what other countries produce large quantities of silk, and what country consumes the most. Examine the specimens in the museum and go to the studio and ask Miss Baily to show how silk is woven. Your art assignment has to do with textiles and dyeing this month. This is particularly interesting.

NOTE: Some of you will remember attending the Silk Show at the Grand Central Palace last spring. Mr. Eaton of the Nonotuck Silk Company is sending us some silk-worms so that you can observe them at work.

Equivalents

The reading of problem 1 will count as two days' work; answering the questions in problem 1 will count as one day's work; problem 2 will count as two days' work.

4th Week

Problems

I am giving you a choice of subjects for research work. Select either "The Chinese Boy" or "The Chinese Girl." As you proceed with your reading you will understand how to connect the subheadings, which I am about to suggest, with the subject you have selected.

The Chinese Boy.
Ancestor Worship
Education
Chinese Writing
Examinations
The Mandarin
The Chinese Girl.
She is not wanted—why?
Foot-binding
Clothes
Polygamy
The Mother-in-Law

Refer to any books on China. Look in the index for what you want.

There are some interesting pictures of Chinese life and noted Chinese men in the History Laboratory. The Thursday conference will be in the nature of a debate. The boys may take the side of the Chinese boy, and the girls the side of the Chinese girl. *Question:* China is the best place in the world in which to be educated.

Equivalents

The reading of your topic will count as two days' work; the writing as three days' work.

Assignment No. 2

(For Seventh Grade Pupils of 11 to 12 years.)

Grade VII　　　　　　*4th Contract Assignment*

GEOGRAPHY

Topic: South America.

You are commissioned by the Secretary of Commerce of the United States Government to visit

South America and report on the commercial resources and possibilities of that continent.

1st Week

Before starting on your journey you will probably wish to familiarize yourself somewhat with the maps of South America.

Problems

PROBLEM 1. Make a political map of South America showing the equator, the zones, the principal rivers and mountain ranges.

PROBLEM 2. Compare the positions of North America and South America with regard to the equator, the poles, longitudes, other continents.

PROBLEM 3. Compare the coast lines of the two continents. Which is poor in harbours?

PROBLEM 4. Consult the steamship folders on South America and decide on a route which will enable you to visit all the important countries of South America, including Bolivia. In Brazil you may find it necessary to visit two or three cities in order to bring back an all-inclusive report to the Secretary of Commerce.

NOTE: Instead of a conference this week we are all going to Central Park to witness the unveiling of the Statue "Bolivar" by two of our children Patricia and Maraquita MacManus whose great grandfather was the first President of Bolivia. It is interesting to us all to know that this statue is the work of Peggy's modelling teacher.

PROBLEM 5. For a brief account of the history of

South America read pp. 203-205 in Tarr and
McMurry. Book II.

Report orally on Problems 2, 3, 4 and 5.

Equivalents

Problem 1 will count as two days' work; Problems 2 and 3 as a day's work; Problem 4 as one day's work; Problem 5 as one day's work.

2nd Week

You are now ready to start on your journey.

Problems

PROBLEM 1.   I suggest that you make only short
visits to Venezuela and the Guianas, noting only
the chief products and the climatic peculiarities.

PROBLEM 2.   The United States is deeply interested in the actual and potential resources of
Brazil.   Ascertain at the several ports what products are being exported, in what quantities.

PROBLEM 3.   Learn as much about the valley of
the Amazon as possible.   Inform yourself on the
subject of rubber.

References

You will find information that will enable you
to interpret your experiences in some of the following books:—

Geography of Commerce and Industry—Robinson.

American Educator.
Man and His Work—Herbertson.
Advanced Geography.
Tarr and McMurry. Book II.
Story of Rubber—John Martin.

Written Work

Take notes for your own use on each problem.

Equivalents

Problem 1 (with notes) will count as one day's work; Problem 2 as two days' work; Problem 3 as two days' work.

3rd Week

Continue your journey and conclude it.

Problems

PROBLEM 1. Make only brief visits to Uruguay and Paraguay.

PROBLEM 2. Visit Argentine, making detailed inquiries as you did in Brazil.

PROBLEM 3. Visit Peru and Chile, making detailed inquiries as before and investigating the influence of the Andes Mountains upon the climate of these countries.

PROBLEM 4. Make a short visit to Colombia to ascertain whether there are any prospective oil fields there.

References

See last week's assignment.

Written Work

Take notes as you did last week.

Equivalents

Problems 1 and 4 will count as one-half a day's work each; Problems 2 and 3 as two days' work each.

4th Week

The Secretary expects to receive your report by the 10th. It should be based on your notes and should comprise not less than ten closely written pages.

Equivalents

Two or more pages will count as one day's work. The report will not be considered complete, however, unless all your notes have been embodied in it.

ASSIGNMENT No. 3

(For High School Pupils of 13 to 14 years.)

High School GEOGRAPHY
1st Year   *4th Contract Assignment*

We have worked for some time on problems suggested by the Conference on Disarmament with special reference to China and Japan. We are now about to take up some of the same problems and many new ones, from the viewpoint of Imperial Britain.

1st Week

Problems

PROBLEM 1. Read in the New World, by Isaiah Bowman—a recent and authoritative book on political geography—Chapter II on "Problems of Imperial Britain, pp. 12-16, the introductory paragraphs in which the extent of the British Empire and the gains resulting from the Great War are discussed. The entire Chapter runs from p. 12—p. 79.

It will be worth your while to take rather full notes.

PROBLEM 2. On p. 31 of Practical Map Exercises, Eastern Hemisphere, you will find a map of the world. Trace this map. List the parts of the British Empire as classified on p. 29 of The New World. Locate these parts on the map, using neat printed abbreviations or corresponding numbers rather than whole words.

You will find a map of the world with the British Empire shown in red in Lyde's Economic Atlas. In Rand & McNally's Atlas of Reconstruction you will find what additions have been made to the Empire since 1914.

Equivalents

Problem 1 will count as three days' work; Problem 2 as two days' work.

2nd Week

Problems

PROBLEM 1. In the New World read carefully (taking notes as usual) pp. 16-27 on The Trade

Organization of the Empire and the paragraphs on p. 28 which deal with the policies of Great Britain towards the parts of her Empire.

PROBLEM 2. Supplement your notes with a one-page discussion of one of the following subjects:—

The relation of coal to industry.

The points of resemblance between England and Japan.

Free trade and protection as national policies.

Equivalents

Problem 1 will count as three days' work; Problem 2 as two days' work.

3rd Week

The five self-governing dominions—Canada, Australia, South Africa, New Zealand and New-foundland—constitute a bulwark rather than a menace to the British Empire. Yet they are not entirely satisfied with their large measure of freedom, as you will read on pp. 29-30 of The New World, by Bowman.

The most acute problems confronting Great Britain arise (according to Bowman, who evidently considers South Africa from two distinct standpoints) from these portions of the empire wherein an intense nationalism threatens revolution:—Ireland, South Africa, India, and Egypt. Since the writing of this book an agreement has been reached between English and Irish delegates which apparently solves the problem of Ireland. The circumstances and terms in the New World, taking detailed notes. (This account of the Irish

question seems lacking in several particulars.)
Find out about:—
1. The great Irish leaders of the Nineteenth Century.
2. The Sinn Fein Party.

Equivalents

The reading and notes will count as three days' work; the questions discussed with me will count as two days' work.

4th Week

Bring to school any books or magazines you can find that contain accounts of the Irish controversy, or of the agreement recently arrived at. I will bring anything I can find.

Decide what aspect of the question interests you most, and assign yourself a definite amount of reading.

Write a paper of say, 3 pages, from the Ulster, British, or Sinn Fein point of view. Stress radical, religious, political or economic differences, as seems best to you. You will be given credit for this paper in the English department. The best one will be read in assembly on Wednesday.

NOTE: Mr. Seumas MacManus, the Irish writer, will be at the school on Tuesday. He will attend your conference the third week. On Tuesday of the fourth week Mr. Humphrey (who is well known in political circles and who officiated at the opening of Sulgrave Manor) will take up any side of the Irish controversy on which you may desire to question him. It may be interesting for you to talk with Tom, the Scotch carpenter, who has some decided views.

MATHEMATICS ASSIGNMENT

ASSIGNMENT No. 1.

(For Eighth Grade Pupils of 12 to 13 years.)

Grade VIII   *5th Contract Assignment*
MATHEMATICS

It often happens that a business undertaking may be too large for one or two individuals to supply all the money which may be needed, and so a number of persons unite and form what is called a *stock company* or *corporation.* For instance, you would like $50.00 or more for your "Puppet Theatre." We shall suppose that all who are in Grades VII and VIII were to form a stock company and agree to take a certain number of shares.

We shall call the stock company the "Puppet Theatre Corporation." Edgar will be the company's agent, so he will sell the shares. He will be furnished with some blank certificates, so you may come to him for shares.

The company's capital will amount to $50.00 and each share will be valued at $1.00. If Alice buys 10 shares she will have to pay $10.00. It will be Edgar's business to sell his shares in such a way that all members of Grades VII and VIII may be shareholders.

A company's profits are called its *dividends* and

are divided at regular periods among the shareholders according to the number of shares each possesses.

Stock is not money, but it can be bought and sold for money, and a shareholder can get money for his stock only by selling it to some person who is willing to buy. The *par value* is the real value of each share. Stocks are *at a discount,* or *at a premium,* according as the shares sell for below or above their par value.

1st Week

STOCKS. We shall now have some problems on the buying and selling of these stocks.

Bulletin Study

On the bulletin board in the mathematics room you will find a list containing the names of the pupils who have bought shares. This list will also indicate the number of shares they have bought.

Problems

1. Find out how much annual dividend Gretchen would receive from her shares at $4\frac{1}{2}\%$ per year.

2. Find the annual dividends of all the shareholders if the rate is 5% per year.

3. How much $2\frac{1}{2}\%$ stock must Eugene hold in order to obtain an annual income of $1.00?

4. How many shares at $56\frac{1}{2}\%$ could he buy for $30.00?

5. Elizabeth Sandler sells 6 of her "Puppet

Theatre'' shares at 35% and invests the proceeds in bank stock at $.45. How many shares of bank stock does she buy?

6. Work questions 8, 9, 10 on page 245 and questions 2, 3, 4, 5 on page 244 of the Ontario Public School Arithmetic.

Written Work

As usual, you will work these problems in your note-books.

Conference

During our conference, which fortunately comes early in the week, Edgar will sell his stock. We shall make out a list of the shares sold, ready to post on the bulletin board.

Equivalents

Problems 1 and 2 count for one day's work; Problems 3, 4 and 5 count for one day's work: Problem 6 counts as three days' work.

2nd Week

INTEREST.

Interest is the money paid for the use of money.

The *Principal* is the sum of money on which the interest is charged.

The *Amount* is the sum due at maturity. It contains both principal and interest.

The *rate* is the number of per cent of the principal in the yearly interest.

References

Read carefully paragraph 390 on page 184 of "The New Practical Arithmetic."

Problems

Work the problems given under 391.

You will notice that it asks for the interest on these different sums at 6% for 60 days, 30 days, 90 days, 6 days, 12 days, 18 days, 3 days, 2 days, 24 days. Do them in the simplest way possible.

Equivalents

Any four problems count a day's work.

Written Work or Oral Report

You should be able to do a great number of these mentally. The rest may be worked in your notebooks.

Conference

I shall spend the time of this week's conference in explaining the first principles of interest to those of you who have not had any problems in Interest.

3rd Week

REVIEW. We shall devote our time this week to a general review.

Problems

1. A lot is 8.5 rods long and 6.4 rods wide. What decimal part of an acre is it?

2. Change 3/25 to a decimal and divide the result by .25; by 2.5; by 25.

3. What part of a cubic foot is a block 12 inches by 6 inches by 2 inches.

4. How much will it cost to insure a house for $7,200.00, at 3/8%; at 3/10%: at 1/4%?

5. A dealer sold 65% of his stock of lumber and then had 7,000 ft. left: How much lumber had he before the sale?

6. A house worth $4,500.00 is insured for 2/3 of its value at 3/5% what is the premium?

7. What is the interest on $1.00 for 1 year at 6%? For 3 years? For 2½ years?

8. What is the interest on $1.00 for 30 days at 6%? for 6 days? For 18 days? For 24 days?

9. A man who owned 3/4 of a mine sold 1/3 of his share for $2,650.00; at this rate what is the value of the mine?

10. A circle is 14 ft. in diameter. Find the area and the circumference.

11. What is the ratio of 3½ ft. to 10½ ft.? 6 in. to 18 in.? 12½ lbs. to 50 lbs.?

12. What decimal equals 1/4; 3/4; 1/3; 2/3; 1/6; 5/6; 1/8; 3/8; 3/5; 4/5?

13. A girl is 15 years old and her age is 3/10 of the age of her father. How old is her father?

14. How many times will a hoop 7 ft. in diameter turn around in rolling 132 feet? 83 feet?

15. A boy gave 2/5 of his money for a slate and 1/10 of it for a ruler. What part had he left?

Equivalents

Any three questions count as one day's work.

Written Work

Keep a record of these in your note-books. Mark any which you found difficulty in solving.

4th Week

CURVED SURFACES.

You will remember that we worked some easy problems in circles, curved surfaces, etc., during the first week of your 4th assignment.

Problems

These problems are a continuance of the work of the 4th assignment.

PROBLEM. Work the questions in Exercise XIX of Book 1, Philips' Arithmetic.

NOTE: You may choose either this or one of the weeks in Algebra in Part B.

Equivalents

The exercise counts for five days' work.

This completes Part A.

CONFERENCE.

In our conference this week we shall have a general review of the work of the 5th Assignment.

PART B.

Algebra

Part B is not compulsory for all of you, but I should like as many as possible to try it. If you complete parts B and C satisfactorily, you will be marked a "maximum pupil" on your report.

Problems

Will you read very carefully pages 1 and 2 of the General Mathematics.

Problem 1.   What is an equation?

Explain to me either orally or by means of written work how this experiment proves that if the same number be subtracted from both sides of an equation the remainders are equal.

Problem 2.   There is another experiment described on page 3 which proves that if both sides of an equation are divided by the same number the quotients are equal.   Can you explain this also?

Work all the problems on pages 2 and 4.

Equivalents

Equations.

The parts of an expression separated by plus (+) and minus (—) signs are called the terms of a number.

Thus 2a and 3b are the terms of the number 2a+3b. A one term number is called a monomial.

Problems

PROBLEM 1.

$$8-7-2= \text{?} \qquad 8x-7x-2x= \text{?}$$
$$8+2-7= \text{?} \qquad 8x+2x-7x= \text{?}$$
$$2+8-7= \text{?} \qquad 2x+8x-7x= \text{?}$$

The value of an expression is unchanged if the order of its terms is changed, provided each term carries with it the sign at its left. If no sign is expressed at the left of the first term of an expression the plus sign is understood.

SIMILAR AND DISSIMILAR TERMS.

Terms which have a common literal factor, as $2x$, $3x$ and $5x$, are *similar terms*. Their sum is a one-term expression, namely, $10x$. When terms do not have a common literal factor, as $2x$ and $3y$, they are called *dissimilar terms*.

Algebraic expressions are simplified by combining similar terms. Combining similar terms in either the right or the left member of an equation gives us the same equation in simpler form.

PROBLEM 2.   Solve the following equations:

1. $2x-7=x+3$.
2. $3x+2=x+8$.
3. $5x-3x+2x-2=2x+x+12$.
4. $16y-8y+3y-2=5y-2y+14$.
5. $20+4x=38-10x$.
6. $5x+3-x=x+18$.
7. $7r+18+3r=32+2r-2$.
8. $16+6s+30+6s-4s+8+12+3s+13+s129$.
9. $25y-20-7y-5=56-5y+5$.

Equivalents

Problem 1 counts as one-half a day's work: in Problem 2, two questions count as one day's work.

PART C.

Work the following problems:

PROBLEM 1: A garden roller is 4 ft. 8 in. in circumference, and is 2 ft. 10 in. long. How many square yards of ground would be covered when it has turned 12 times?

PROBLEM 2. The sides of a wooden building 50 ft. long, 18½ ft. wide, and with walls 12½ ft. high, are to be painted. Find the area that is to be so treated.

ART ASSIGNMENTS

ASSIGNMENT No. 1

(For Fifth Grade Pupils of 9 to 10 years.)

Grade V   ART   *3rd Contract Assignment*

CHRISTMAS GIFTS

Block printed mat or magazine cover.

DESIGN.

1. Study the illustrative material—block printed mat and designs and blocks posted on the green bulletin board. Notice the nice, interesting

spacing in the designs—it is not all alike. Notice the interesting edges of the designs. They have variety also.

2. How to begin: Choose the size you wish your design to be and cut out a piece of manilla drawing paper that size. Next decide upon the shape—shall it be a leaf shape or a flower shape. Think about the curves and make them beautiful when you cut them. When you have a large shape so cut that it pleases you, think about the edges. Can you make those edges more interesting? Study again the edges of the designs on the bulletin board. Notice that the edges are decorated in an orderly way. See what you can do to yours.

When your edges have been decorated think of the central part of your design. Here you must consider your spacing quite carefully. Be sure that you have variety, and be sure that the shape of the centre design looks well with the outside shape. Use a dark paper for this part of the design. Arrange your design carefully, and bring it to me for criticism.

The making of your design is one week's work. HOW TO MAKE YOUR BLOCK.

Trace your design onto a piece of thin white tracing paper by drawing around each part of it. If you do not understand, ask me to show you how to do it.

When your design is well traced, get a piece of linoleum the right size from me, put a thin coat of paste all over your linoleum, and spread your tracing paper on top. With a newspaper over this, rub carefully with a pencil.

When this has thoroughly dried, you are ready

to cut your block. Ask me to show you how to do it.

This will count for two-and-a-half days' work.

How to put your Design onto your Mat or Magazine Cover.

We call this "blocking the design," or "block printing" it. I will have to show you how to do this, but you may get the following materials before asking me to help you.

> 10 pins, spool of thread, your block print, a ruler, 4 thumb tacks and your linen or silk, a drawing-board and either 4 paper towels or a piece of felt or cotton for padding.

Blocking and making your gift is one-and-a-half weeks' work. That means you have done three weeks' work altogether.

Assignment No. 2

(For Seventh Grade Pupils of 11 to 12 years.)

Grade VII   ART ASSIGNMENT   *3rd Month*

Christmas Gifts

Stencilled Bag or Stencilled Table Centre.

Design.

Materials to work with: Manilla paper, scissors, illustrative material posted on the board or found on the brown table.

The design itself: Study carefully the illustrative material. Notice the variety of shapes, the interesting shapes, the fact that either the dark or the light is most important, the fact that your background must be interesting as well as your foreground, and that it all holds together, making a single unit or design.

How to begin: Choose the shape and size you wish your motif to be. Decide whether it shall be a leaf or a flower motif. Fold your paper in half (after you have cut it the correct size), then open it out before beginning to cut out your design.

Your design: Study your paper and see if you can find a design in it. Work on just half of your paper first, then folding it, make the other half like the first. Cut the general shape first, either leaf or flower. Then begin to work out a design for the centre, thinking carefully about the dark and light shapes. Be sure to have variety and beautiful line. Bring your design to me for criticism. Cut design from stencil paper.

APPLICATION OF DESIGN.

Ask me to show you how to do the stencilling. Choose carefully the size and proportion of your bag and table runner. Decide just where your design is to go. Your design may be used as a border on either the bag or table runner. Try repeating it on paper at different distances apart to see which looks the best. Try to have the space between your designs make an interesting shape. When you have planned your repeats let me see the arrangement before you put it on the material.

Materials you will need for stencilling: Pins, thread, stencil brush, paint, silk or linen for your Christmas gift.

MUSIC ASSIGNMENT

Assignment No. 1

(For Sixth Grade Pupils of 10 to 11 years.)

Grade VI MUSIC *5th Contract Assignment*

1st Week

READING.

We will continue our study of folk songs. Choose two songs from the list we made last month and study in this way:

1. What is the pulse? Clap the rhythm. What are the rhythmic patterns?

2. Find the melodic patterns; write these in your music notebook and mark the number of times each appears. Sing the first phrase. Sing the second phrase, and so on through the song.

3. Where is the home-tone? Spell the major scale from that tone. Spell the major chord from that tone. Are there any phrases made entirely from tones of that chord?

4. Play the song on the piano (melody only). Can you play it in another key?

5. Write the song from memory in your notebook. Re-write it in another key.

The above will count as five days' work.

2nd Week

SINGING.

1. Study exercises Nos. 21, 22, 23, and 24 in your solfege book. Do not mark your card until we have sung these in our conference.

Three days' work.

2. We will devote part of our conference time to the learning of these songs: (*a*) All the Birds have Come Again; (*b*) Early One Morning; (*c*) Now the Day is Over.

Memorizing the words will count for two days' work.

3rd Week

RHYTHM.

1. Divide the following exercises into measures, indicated by the pulse signature, and sing them on any one pitch, as *do, mi*.

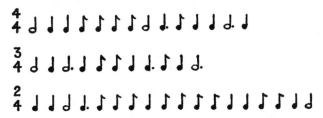

This will count as one day's work.

2. Scan the words of the song "Lady Moon." Draw the note heads, the pulse signature, and the bars. Be sure all measures are filled.

Three days' work.

3. Here are the first phrases of folk songs you know. Do you recognize them? When you are sure you do, put in pulse signatures and bars and the words represented here.

One day's work.

You should be able to recognize rhythms through the ear and to reproduce them in written symbols. Our ear training drills will help you to do this.

4th Week

HARMONY.

Harmonize one of the folk songs you studied under READING.

Two days' work.

HISTORY.

In your English work this month you are going to write about the life of some great musician. You will find on the bulletin board in the music room pictures of musicians about whom we have studied, also a list of questions concerning these musicians which will help you to remember the points we discussed in our study.

The work in English will count as two days' work in music.

Vocabulary.

The composer marks his composition "adagio": how will you play it? Will a cradle song be played piano or forte?

One day's work.

CHAPTER VII

WHEN we first began to put the Dalton Laboratory
Plan into operation the pupils were given a daily
diary in which they were expected to enter the
amount of work they had done in each subject before leaving any laboratory. But this method, besides imposing a great deal of extra reading upon
the teacher, soon proved itself inadequate to the
purpose. At the same time it was evident that some
measure of time and work was essential. Frequently pupils who had worked steadily were surprised to find themselves behindhand with their
contract job at the end of the week. Without a
check to show them exactly what they had done
they were, we found, apt to devote too much time
to a favourite subject and not enough to the
others. Often, indeed, they wandered altogether
from the assigned requirements and even from the
subjects indicated therein. The time allotted was
being used without any real sense of responsibility. Comprehension of what that responsibility
entailed was lacking. As long as time was not
consciously wasted pupils failed at that moment
to grasp that the proper division of their time was
essential to the good and satisfactory use of it.
They were like people who expect you to pardon

their errors of judgment on consideration of their good intentions. They did not budget time, they merely squandered it.

I have already related my early experiments when the graph method of checking progress first occurred to me. Its superiority to the diary soon became evident, and henceforward it was adopted as an integral portion of the Dalton Plan. This device not only helps the pupil to measure his time wisely, but also to adjust it to the fulfilment of his job. It made the contract stand out clearly as a whole unit, and imparted a sense of responsibility without driving the pupil. But the graph has done more than that. It has lightened the teacher's task and simplified the organization of work in the laboratories and the general organization of the school.

There are three different kinds of graphs. The first is the Instructor's Laboratory Graph, which is kept in the laboratory under the direction of the specialist in charge. These graphs are printed in five or more colours, one for each of the different forms. The following sample, like all my graphs, is made by the Educational Supply Association, 40A Holborn Viaduct, London, and can be procured in the United States through the Children's University School.

This sample Graph I assumes that there are thirty-five pupils in the class. I have filled in a few names in order to illustrate clearly the method of marking progress. Mary, Clara, Dorothy, and Helen have, we will suppose, finished the work required during the first week of the monthly assignment. Each girl, therefore, draws a line opposite to her name through the five spaces to indicate the work accomplished. These five spaces represent five days' work. Frances, having only done two-fifths of the week's work, draws her line across two of the five spaces, while Mildred and Anne record their three-fifths in the same way. The equivalents indicated in the assignment show them how to reckon their work.

By this method the instructor can tell at a glance exactly what progress each pupil has made in any given subject, and by consulting the graphs in the other laboratories she can follow his progress in all the subjects of his contract. The graph also shows which subjects are most interesting to the child, and to what extent the assignment affects the development of the class as a whole.

On the other hand, it is equally valuable to the pupil who is conscious every time he marks the graph, both of what work he has done and of what remains to do. He can, at the same time, compare his achievement with that of his fellow pupils. Of course, the quick, intelligent child will make, at least in some subjects, more rapid progress than the slow or stupid child. But having checked his progress himself, he has no sense of unfairness in the estimation of his powers. The graph eliminates the discouraging feeling of being at a disadvantage in comparison with others, which is so afflicting to a slow child under the class system. Very often, too, the pupil, who is abnormally slow in some subjects, is shown by the graph method to be abnormally quick in some one subject for which he has a natural aptitude. By budgeting his time he can make better progress in getting ahead.

INSTRUCTOR'S LABORATORY GRAPH.																								
SUBJECT History.				FORM VI		ASSIGNMENT I					INSTRUCTOR R N B.													
NAMES				1ST WEEK				2ND WEEK					3RD WEEK					4TH WEEK						
		1	2	3	4	5	6	7	8	9	10	11	12	13	14	15	16	17	18	19	20		
1	Mary. B.																						
2	Louise C.																						
3	Clara. B.																						
4	Frances M.																						
5	Dorothy S.																						
6	Mildred W.																						
7	Helen K.																						
8	Anne P																						
9	etc..																						
10																							
11																							
12																							
13																							
14																							
15																							
16																							
17																							
18																							
19																							
20																							
21																							
22																							
23																							
24																							
25																							
26																							
27																							
28																							
29																							
30																							
31																							
32																							
33																							
34																							
35																							

Dalton Graph, No. 1. Copyright, Children's University School.

GRAPH I

(Actual size: 12 by 8 in.)

Graphs are, moreover, very helpful to a teacher in the choice of the right moment to offer special help or instruction to her pupils. If, for instance, she observes that several children have reached the same stage in their work on any given subject, she can give them an appointment to meet her together on the following day at a fixed hour in the laboratory belonging to that subject. These appointments should be posted on the students' general notice board. Any individual or group, or, if advisable, the entire class, can be summoned in this way for help and consultation. Experience has shown us that students appreciate these calls.

We come now to graph II, or, as it is called, the Pupil's Contract Graph, whereby a student can watch and record his progress in all the subjects of his assignment. Each time he marks the laboratory graph as I have described he makes a corresponding line for that subject upon his own particular graph. It is, as it were, a balance sheet of his time. Before beginning work, every morning he ought to study it carefully, for it automatically reminds him both of his weakness in some subjects and of the time which he should set aside to overcome that weakness. The Pupil's Contract Graph has, we find, done more than anything to inculcate the value of time and a sense of responsibility for its use. It has also generated a spontaneous desire to save time so that special difficulties should be conquered. These graphs stimulated thorough work rather than hurried work. The pupil's graph is printed in different colours corresponding to the laboratory graphs.

Most of the headings and spaces on the sample

THE PUPIL'S CONTRACT GRAPH

					NAME OF SCHOOL		DATE BEGUN	
NAME Betty Underwood					Childrens University School		October 5th	
ADDRESS 10 West 72nd Street					**AGE** 12	**NUMBER OF CONTRACT ASSIGNMENT** I.	**DATE COMPLETED** November 1st	**No OF WEEKS** 4.
					FORM II.			**No OF DAYS**
								ABSENT

SUBJECTS	Mathematics	History	Geography	English	Science	French
TESTS	A	A	B	A	A	B

Week values (by assignment number):

Week	Mathematics	History	Geography	English	Science	French
4TH WEEK	18. 19.	18. 19.	18. 19. 20.	19. 20.	19. 20.	14.
3RD WEEK	15.	18.	10.	12.	15.	11.
2ND WEEK	13. 14.	9.	9.	6.	7.	9. 10.
1ST WEEK		1.	3.	4. 5.	1.	8.
						4.

Dalton Graph, No. 1. Copyright, Children's University School.

GRAPH II

(Actual size: 9 by 5½ in.)

pupil's graph explain themselves, but a brief explanation of how it is to be used as a record is necessary. It will be seen that at the bottom of the card, ten spaces are provided for the names of the maximum number of subjects a pupil can carry. Under these spaces there are similar blanks against the word "Test." This word can, of course, be interpreted in various ways. I do not myself believe that examinations supply any real test of a pupil's knowledge or ability. But the word and the space have been included in the graph for the use of such schools as hold periodical examinations.

The four spaces marked "1st week, 2nd week, 3rd week, 4th week" correspond to the four weekly assignments or divisions of any monthly contract. In order to indicate the days in a school week each weekly partition has five separate spaces. This makes it possible for a pupil who has, let us suppose, done three-fifths of a week's work in mathematics to draw an upward line through three of the five spaces. If he has only completed half a week's work he should draw the line through two-and-a-half spaces.

Betty Underwood is twelve years of age, a pupil in Form II, who begins her contract job on October 5th. Only major subjects are entered in her graph, and in this, her first assignment, she carries Mathematics, History, Geography, English, Science, and French. Being a voluntary agent in the use of her time, Betty decides on her first day to study history. She therefore goes into the history laboratory and stays there until she has exhausted her interest in the history part of her assignment and desires a change of subject. Before leaving it she consults the teacher in charge and ascertains that she has done the equivalent in time of three-fifths of a week's work in history. She records this by drawing a line across three spaces on the Instructor's Laboratory Graph, and in her new Pupil Contract Graph she draws another line up through three of the five spaces. At the end of each line she places a figure one (1) to show that it is her first work day on this particular assignment.

Betty then elects to go into the English laboratory. On reading through the English assignment she will find that owing to the varied nature of the work equivalents in time are given. Grammar, she is told, will count for two days' work; reading for two more days; and composition for one day. Being in no mood for composition she decides to read, and does all the reading required in her assignment. As there is still a little time left before twelve o'clock, she attacks her grammar, finishing half of the amount required. Her equivalent is thus one space indicating one day of work for grammar and two spaces or two days, for reading; so after drawing a line through three spaces on the Instructor's Laboratory Graph, she marks the English column on her own graph in the same way.

The entire morning of her second day is spent by Betty in the science laboratory. Consequently, she not only finishes her first week's assignment in science, but also does one day's work of the second week's requirements. To indicate this, she adds the figure ''2'' at the end of the graph line which covers six spaces, showing that the sixth space is included in her second day's work of the first week.

The second sample of Graph II shows Betty's completed contract, the numbers attached to the end of each line indicate the day on which she has done a given piece of work. What we constantly should note is whether or not the children are completing the twenty days' allotted work in twenty days or not.

If Betty had worked for five days and then absented herself through illness, upon the day of her return to school she would have marked everything accomplished with a "6." We do not want her to feel that she has lost ground but rather to measure the ground covered in terms of time taken. In this way we can fairly measure her with her contemporaries.

In reading her graph we see that she has finished her assignment in the allotted twenty days. The figure "4" entered under the heading "No. of weeks" shows this. But if the assignment had taken her twenty-two days she would have added the figure "2" under the heading "No. of days," signifying four weeks and two days for the monthly contract job.

On the nineteenth day, though Betty had completed her first month's work in mathematics, she was not permitted to start the second month's work in this subject, because her contract requires fulfillment in all its parts before taking on extra work in any one part. The object of the Pupil's Contract Graph is only to measure laboratory time, so only assigned subjects should be entered there-

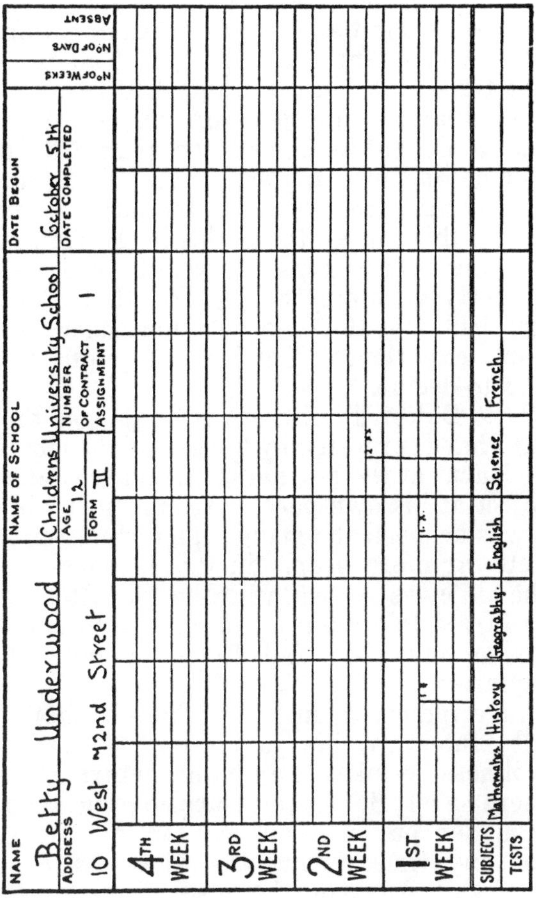

Dalton Graph, No. 1. Copyright, Children's University School. * First day ** Second day

GRAPH II. (Showing completed contract.)

(Actual size: 9 by 5½ in.)

upon. But before Betty terminates her month she will have been submitted to tests or examinations during the concurrent oral lessons. Had these successive tests revealed that Betty had been able to accomplish all her allotted work in, say fifteen days, she could safely have been permitted to tackle her second month's assignment in mathematics, for her general written examination would be fixed with those of all the pupils in the form at the end of the twenty days. It would not be fair to make Betty regulate her pace on that of the slower pupils. But this is a question which each instructor's experience of individual pupils will enable her to decide.

Under the Dalton Plan there is no danger that a child will have forgotten by the end of the month what she learnt at the beginning. Having studied each subject at his own pace at the moment when interest was keenest, the knowledge thus acquired fixes itself far more deeply in the memory than under the old class system, when he was often unwillingly forced to cram a lesson for recitation on the following day, which faded from his mind immediately after.

As I have indicated, in cases where a pupil is obliged to interrupt his job owing to absence through illness he takes it up on his return at the point where he left it. As there are no programme conflicts under our method, he can also enter school at any time during the term. A child simply marks his day on the basis of his accomplishment as he goes on, just as a time contractor is paid for his job whatever it may be according to the number of days he works at it.

From the social point of view we have also found the graph device invaluable. The tendency among members of a form is always to compare their graphs. Elder students also develop interest in, and sympathy with, the progress of the younger children, and frequently help them without any prompting from the teacher with advice on the division of their time and on the best way to overcome difficulties of all kinds. Thus group control and the sentiment of fraternity spreads through the school to the lasting benefit of all concerned.

To become masters not only of their time and work, but also of themselves, is a real preparation for life where we have to learn to do the work that lies before us whether we are interested in it or not. And even interest grows out of the sense of problems solved and obstacles conquered. As a child once remarked to a teacher whom I know: "You learn that whatever you have to do can become what you want to do." That child was not by any means an abnormally intelligent specimen. He was, on the contrary, rather below the average, a boy who had after much struggle and perseverance risen above his natural difficulties. And I think I can claim that it was the Dalton Plan which enabled him to attain self-mastery.

On the back of the Pupil's Contract Graph there is a blank space for a list of suggestions to pupils which can be made either by the staff or by a committee of students. Here they can be told exactly how to use their graphs, and such recommendations as "If you find one laboratory crowded it is advisable to go into another in order to avoid wasting your time'' may be included. Do not, however, let the suggestions degenerate into a list of rules. This can be avoided by allowing students to make suggestions from time to time which will, moreover, stimulate their imagination as well as develop the sense of responsibility. Young children may not be capable of this, but girls and boys between twelve and twenty should certainly be called upon occasionally to make suggestions for their own form.

Graph III is a Form or, as in England, a House Graph in which emphasis is placed upon the entire number of weeks of work done. For convenience it is designed with forty spaces so as to record progress in as many as ten subjects. If six major subjects out of the curriculum are carried by one pupil, then, with four weeks of work to be done in each subject, the total contract will represent twenty-four weeks. Five subjects represent twenty weeks, and so on. Graph III, of which the following is a sample, should be marked every week either at its beginning or at its close. It may be cut to fit the number of weeks required by any contract.

By using a fresh Form or House Graph every week we can get a psychological picture of the general progress of each class and of the whole school. These records should be dated and carefully preserved in its archives. Graph III should contain a space for every pupil in the house or form. We

FORM OR HOUSE GRAPH	ASSIGNMENT	WEEK
Name 7.orm. II.	1.	1st

NAMES	1	2	3	4	5	6	7	8	9	10	11	12	13	14	15	16	17	18	19	20	21	22	23	24	25	26	27	28	29	30	31	32	33	34	35	36	37	38	39	40
1 Betty																																									
2 Mary																																									
3 Helen																																									
4																																									
5																																									
6																																									
7																																									
8																																									
9																																									
10																																									
11																																									
12																																									
13																																									
14																																									
15																																									
34																																									
35																																									

Dalton Graph, No. 3. Copyright, Children's University School.

GRAPH III

(Actual size: 12 by 10½ in.)

Note.—There are spaces for thirty-five pupils, but for conveniences the space for pupils Nos. 16–33 have been omitted from this reproduction.

will continue Betty's story to illustrate how it should be used.

Assuming that she has done, during one weekly period of five days, an equivalent of four days of history, three days of English, and five days of geography, six days of science, and one day of French, or nineteen days in all, we proceed to divide nineteen by five in order to establish how many weeks of work she has completed towards her total. Our result being three and four-fifths,

ATTENDANCE GRAPH

DAY AND DATE Wednesday Feb 1st 1922				
NAMES	A. M.		P. M.	
	ON TIME	LATE	ON TIME	LATE
Betty	✓		✓	
Mary	✓		✓	
Helen		9·10	✓	
etc				

GRAPH IV

Betty is entitled to mark three spaces and the greater part of a fourth space on the Form Graph.

A fourth graph for the registration of attendance is used in some day schools, either one graph for the whole school if it is small, or one for each form if preferred. The Attendance Graph should be posted on the hall notice board so that each pupil can record the hour of her arrival every morning. We have not a printed card for this graph, but it is very simple to design. Under the date is a list of all the children's names, and opposite each two spaces, one headed "Punctual," the other headed "Late." Good timekeepers mark their arrival in the first space, the late ones record the exact time—which they can see on the clock that should hang above the notice board—when they reach school. The absence of any pupil is indicated by the blank space.

CHAPTER VIII

Teaching and Learning

Personally I am of opinion that teaching has been done more efficiently throughout the world than many critics of our educational system realize. Our schools contain a large number of instructors who possess a wide knowledge both of the subjects they teach and of the methods of handling and simplifying that knowledge. If we fail to recognize the high level the teacher frequently attains it is because teaching so often proves ineffective— because the learner does not learn. The truth is that we have hitherto confused the problems of teaching and of learning, or, rather, treated them as if they were not two problems, but one. We have not hitherto appreciated the fact that teaching is simply like taking the horse to the water. It can, on the old system, no more make the learner learn than the leader of the horse can make him drink.

Teachers are not, however, to blame because our school machinery has been carefully built up from the point of view not of pupil, but of the instructor. At best, the most skilful teacher can only erect an educational tent over her class. She may erect it

dramatically in expert fashion, but as the crowd
of pupils assembled under it are individuals who
vary widely in mental and moral equipment, only
a small proportion of them will be able to follow
or to assimilate her efforts. The bulk of them will
find the tent either too small or too large for them.
They will be near to or far from the ''speaker's
idea.'' It is after all her work, not their work;
her speed, not their speed; her interest, not their
interest. Not until learning is envisaged from the
learner's point of view will our youth come out
from school really educated. Not until school machinery is reorganized and the energies of the
pupils released from the time-table and the class-
tent will they begin to develop that initiative, resourcefulness, and concentration which are the indispensable preliminaries to the process of learning.

Under the old system the teacher has become
the chief actor in the play. She is, perhaps uncon-
sciously, occupied in trying to impress her personality and her ideas upon the children. But the
Dalton Plan reverses these parts and gives the
child's personality a chance; the teacher's part
being to accompany the enfolding life step by step.
This is not to relegate the instructor to an inferior
plane. To understand the child and to keep pace
with his growth she must grow herself, for the
same fundamental laws that govern growth prevail on every successive plane.

The true business of school is not to chain the

pupil to preconceived ideas, but to set him free to discover his own ideas and to help him to bring all his powers to bear upon the problem of learning. A contract job upon which he must exercise his ingenuity is in the nature of a challenge to which he responds automatically. Even if at first he does not know quite what to do with his responsibility, experience and freedom together will soon bring understanding. Experience is the best and indeed the only real teacher.

Parents have often asked me why it is that bad language and bad habits wield such a fascination over children. The reason, I believe, is that in adopting them he is conscious and has the joy of acting as a voluntary agent. As such he often seizes upon and forms a habit which no amount of punishment will divest him of. The attraction lies not so much in the evil thing, itself, but in the symbol of freedom which it represents. Thus he delights in the sense of liberty his voluntary adoption of it gives him. Why not let him have this same sensation in connection with work and learning?

"At what age," I have also been asked, "does a child become sufficiently conscious of his experiences to profit by them?" I am inclined to think that at nine or ten the normal child is capable of appreciating his experiences, and that he should then begin to learn to organize his work on that basis. He ought, at that age, to be ready for his first job. Certain facts must, however, be kept in

mind in any consideration of a child's educational
needs. There are, roughly speaking, three separate periods of development which should be taken
into account. Up to the age of eight the child
should be allowed such freedom as will develop his
individual powers so that he can function later as
a responsible member of the group. This is the
reason for, and the purpose of, freedom. During
the second, or pre-adolescent, period, between
eight and twelve, he must acquire the "tools of
knowledge." These will prepare him for adolescence, between twelve and twenty, which is the
third stage in his development. This last, owing
to the physical change it brings, is the most difficult, from the point of view of work and concentration. Unless we help the child to build up its
character in the pre-adolescent period there is a
danger of his following the line of least resistance
during the critical years of adolescence because he
will not have sufficient intellectual ballast.

Liberty is at all ages equally vital to the child,
for he is as truly an individual in infancy as at any
later stage of his life. The Dalton Laboratory
Plan is designed as a step towards the solution of
those problems which are peculiar to the second
and third periods of his evolution.

In infant schools where freedom of work is prac-
tised, the teacher prepares and presents a grada-
tion of stimuli in the form of material objects.
The careful presentation of these objects at the
time when they appeal to the child is enough to

lead him, step by step, through the various subjects of a curriculum. It is evident that at this stage the teacher is really the controlling lever. The extent of control and the benefit derived by the child is determined by the character of the material objects placed in his environment.

At the pre-adolescent stage of a child's life the problem changes with his growth. Now, in addition to freedom and a selected equipment, the pupil should begin to play a part in initiating and organizing his own pursuits. His released energy and intelligence must be used to achieve some purpose of which he is really conscious. Here the extent of his achievement depends upon his ability to organize not only his studies and his equipment, but his time to better and better advantage. This means organizing his life, then and thereafter. In infancy, the power of concentration is shown by prolonged attention, whereas in pre-adolescence concentration is apt to become of shorter duration, but of much higher power. The pupil then requires another kind of freedom. At the earlier stage environment was so conditioned as to control and develop him, now he should continue his development by learning to control his environment. If he is not permitted to do this the power he generates at this age may control him unless he learns to control it.

Modern psychology and its discoveries throw much light upon pre-adolescent problems. It teaches us to replace the inductive methods, dear to the old school of pedagogy, by deductive methods. We have now learnt that a general idea of the thing to be accomplished is essential, not only for the fundamental purpose of arousing the child's interest, but also so that he may intellectually appreciate the purpose of the demands made upon him. The goal to be aimed at is to the child like a carrot to a donkey—it keeps him moving onwards. A project ahead, provided for in terms of a contract job, is the best illustration of the deductive method. When the child has a project in front of him, which he has determined to carry out, his interest may be temporarily, but is never permanently, side-tracked. The same thing holds good in adult life. Without projects it would not be worth living, nor should we be able to live it to any purpose.

Until the Dalton Laboratory Plan showed the new and better way many teachers, while cherishing a theoretical faith in freedom for the child, seem never to have discovered how to reconcile this idea with the task of carrying out a curriculum. They have regarded the problem as if it consisted of two irreconcilable elements instead of realizing that only by liberating the pupil can the curriculum ever be thoroughly and satisfactorily carried out. The new method demonstrates this unity, and in so doing changes the attitudes of both teacher and pupil towards the work to be done and towards each other.

If the curriculum is gradually mastered by the

liberated pupil in his pre-adolescent period, he will possess a body of correlated knowledge which will serve as a ballast for adolescence. Armed with the "tools of knowledge," that stage may be productive of wider powers for building a superstructure of real culture upon a sure foundation. Without this fundamental basis he will have nothing but sand to build upon and may even lose the desire to build altogether.

But modern psychology can help us still more in the testing of individual capacity among pupils. If such tests do not cure the weakness of children who are subjected to them they do reveal those weaknesses very clearly. On one occasion an eminent psychologist applied a series of such tests to pupils in a large secondary school in England. They showed that the students varied enormously in their mental power. The discovered individual capacity was recorded by a number known as the "intelligence quotient," or, as scientists call it, the "I.Q." In this instance it ranged from high to low, but, strange to say, the academic accomplishment of these pupils was not found to correspond to their intelligence quotient. Many pupils with a low "I.Q." far excelled the achievements of others with a high "I.Q." This demonstrated that the conditions prevailing in that school were not calculated to permit mentally superior students to do justice to their capacity. Fourteen months later, after the school had been reorganized on the Dalton Plan, a similar test was made. To my great satisfaction the tests revealed that the most intelligent students had, through this method, attained the highest accomplishment worthy of their powers, the lowest accomplishment coinciding with the lowest intelligence quotient. I strongly recommend school principals to have recourse to these psychological tests—which should, of course, be applied by an expert unconnected with the establishment—both before the adoption of the Dalton Plan and again a year after it has been put into operation. If at the end of the second year the test were again applied, and revealed a failure on the part of any individual pupil to do work commensurate with his "I.Q.," then that pupil should be regarded as an abnormal case for whom a special curriculum should be devised. His failure will probably be traced to some defect of health or character.

Of course, schools, like individuals, possess differences, and occasionally very marked differences, of character and personality. Some will therefore be slower than others to adapt themselves to the new organization. But the difficulty found in adjusting the school collectively to the fresh angle of vision is merely proof of the great necessity of the change. Patience is essential in getting over the transition period. When an automobile is being overhauled the machine is at a standstill. It is the same with a pupil struggling with the new freedom the new plan gives him. While a child is striving to master an inert or a disorderly mind, he will, to all appearances, be at a standstill like the motor. Only when he has learnt how to work will he begin to make progress, but once in good working condition his speed and efficiency should be evident. I have come in contact with many pupils of excellent ability who, after four years of school had very poor records of accomplishment. This failure could almost invariably be traced to the fact that such pupils had habitually used their energy and intelligence to avoid work and to create discord in the school. Several months were required to correct these habits. But as soon as their natural talents were redirected under the Dalton Plan I have often noticed that children who were formerly recalcitrant came out best in the end and surpassed all rivals. I may also add that those teachers who, at the beginning, were doubtful of, and even hostile to, the new method, frequently became its most enthusiastic supporters. A little tact in the inauguration of the change will conjure many of the initial difficulties. Do not introduce it to the pupils with a long sermon on the amount of good it will do them. The best way is to explain it as simply as possible, taking care that its mechanism, especially as regards the graphs, is thoroughly understood. It is advisable, moreover, to proceed by degrees. Instructors should first of all learn to make assignments. Let at least one month elapse before making any experiment in interaction of groups, which means socialization. When the pupils are thoroughly conversant with the new plan of individual work, an interaction of groups in two or three laboratories where the teachers are eager and expert may be attempted. Later on, such co-operation can be extended so as to embrace the whole school.

In the beginning there will probably be a wide divergence in the time spent by each individual in the completion of his contract. To a certain extent this can be regulated by dividing the assignment into minimum, medium, and maximum, as I have already indicated in a previous chapter. The Dalton Plan, when put into operation, will gradually reveal the different rates of speed and capacity of the different pupils. Regular examinations are usually found to be unnecessary after a time for the generality of students. I have found in the instance of younger children that it is useful to set apart fifteen minutes each morning to enable pupils to collect their ideas and their materials before settling down to work, and also to report, say, on two mornings out of the five to their class or house adviser, for consultation on the use of time to be distributed to eliminate a subject difficulty. The matter of oral lessons must largely be left to the judgment of each instructor, and to her knowledge of the individual pupils. I would like, however, to impress upon all instructors the necessity of abandoning the old idea of trying to keep the class or form together. It is a fallacy which, in view of the difference of speed and ability in pupils, has never been, and can never be, a reality. Five pupils can no more be kept together than forty, and the sooner teachers get rid of this illusion which haunts the minds of some of them the better it will be for the school. Keeping together implies coercion, and the chief aim of the Dalton Plan is to abolish coercion in any shape. It envisages as much the liberation of the teacher as the liberation of the child.

Under it, both should function to better advantage. Her more intimate observation of child nature and the importation of pleasure and interest into the lives and work of the children should wield an immense expansive influence upon the personality of the teacher. She will no longer be engaged in thrusting information down unwilling throats, or in exacting uninteresting tasks from apathetic pupils. From being the pursuer the teacher becomes, under the Dalton Plan, the pursued, whose advice and sympathy is sought and valued. And this change of relationship is reflected not only in the success and happiness of the children, but also in the success and happiness of the teacher.

In order to give concrete illustrations of this change of attitude I asked seven instructors all in the same school to state frankly their opinion on the new plan, and what it means to each of them. In this particular school the plan has been for two years in operation, and none of the teachers had any idea of writing for publication.

The history man wrote as follows:

"When I came to teach under the Dalton Laboratory Plan two years ago, with ten years' experience in the regulation schools behind me, I approached my new problems with great interest, but not without some wonder and doubt as to the merits of the new plan. I went into it with eyes open, eager to find therein a better means of training the child and making him a better citizen.

"One of the first things I discovered was that under the Dalton Plan I could arouse much more interest and enthusiasm for history in the children than under the old system. This was because the children went at their work, seeing beforehand the whole job and the purpose of it all. The monthly assignments did that. I can still remember how I hated history when I was at school myself, how I loathed the thought of reading "the next seven pages," not having any idea what I was moving towards! Under the Dalton Plan the children do know what they are moving towards, and I find that the children, without exception, are actively interested in history. Such interest on the child's part begets enthusiasm on the part of the teacher to make his assignments more attractive than ever, and to build up a lasting enthusiasm for the subject.

"The Dalton Laboratory Plan gives a teacher a great opportunity to know the child, an opportunity which he can never get in dealing with a class, no matter how much he tries. Here the teacher is more the big brother and friend than he is a preceptor or instructor. He deals with a child individually, and so gets more intimately acquainted with him. The teacher is merely one member of the social circle, and the child goes to him with problems to talk over just as one person in a community goes to an older friend. There is a wonderful opportunity for the teacher in this, and also a wonderful responsibility.

"The problem of discipline is greatly simplified under the plan. Where the child is impelled to his work by interest, he will naturally be a better citizen in his school than where he is trying to 'put something over' on his arch enemy, the teacher. Of course, in the beginning there is sometimes a thoughtless child who disturbs and upsets the equilibrium of his neighbours, just as such individuals are always found in a community. Pupils of this sort are cared for and put in their places by public opinion among their fellows. Disciplinary action by the teacher becomes rare.

"The Dalton Laboratory Plan means to me a blessed relief from the deadly routine of the class-room and a great opportunity to study individuals and by learning their needs to help them to develop into strong characters and useful citizens." R. W. B., History Instructor.

The geography mistress sent this statement: "If I were asked what feature of the Dalton Laboratory Plan appeals to me most, I should specify the co-operative relation between pupil and teacher which develops under it. Every child in my department now appears to me as an interesting and sympathetic person, with qualities and capacities of which, in many cases, I should hardly have suspected the existence. The children, on the other hand, regard the teacher as a friendly expert engaged with them upon a highly important piece of work.

"The denial of the creative impulse of the worker in the interest of cheap quantity production, and the sharp class barriers erected between employer and employee have their counterparts in the school of to-day. The adoption of the Dalton Plan, after a period of academic and autocratic teaching, might almost be compared to a return to the Mediaeval Guild System with democratic intercourse between master and apprentice, and respect for work as the corner-stone.

"It would be a mistake, however, to assume that less ground is covered under the Dalton Plan than under the old system. The reverse is generally the case, because the children are stimulated by the assumption of responsibility to greater effort. The plan does not pretend to lend itself to the hasty covering of an elaborate curriculum, nor to the acquisition of large amounts of pre-digested intellectual food." L. R.

The science man expresses himself as follows: "In working under the Dalton Plan the teacher finds himself confronted with an experience that is both new and pleasing. He finds to his surprise that the majority of pupils approach their work with an interest and enthusiasm which, under the old system, was confined to a very small minority. The teacher's former rôle of the driver who handed out bits of pre-digested information has changed. He now becomes the true helper whose advice is sought on many and varied problems which are very real to the children. They are no longer working to escape his criticism, or to receive his plaudits, but rather toward the accomplishment of a definite task. Each child feels that the work of all is his own particular task, and the teacher becomes his councillor who will help him to achieve it. This spirit of enthusiasm is contagious, and the laggards are usually carried along with it. This is, perhaps, the first impression that the instructor receives who works for the first time under the Dalton Plan, and, as in the case of the children, his enthusiasm is whetted at the start." R. D. O.

The English mistress is equally appreciative:

"1. The Dalton Plan offers the advantages of individual work. It leads to an understanding of the child and an appreciation of his difficulties.

"2. A feeling of sympathy and friendship between teacher and child is established. The child comes to consider the teacher a helper and friend, and approaches her with many of his own problems.

"3. There is real joy in working with spontaneous children. The plan creates spontaneity.

"4. The work is stimulating. Each individual presents his work in a different way, and this releases the teacher from a monotonous and set method of teaching.

"5. The actual writing of assignments each month tends to systematize the plan of work.

"6. The teacher has an opportunity to devote her time and energy to teaching because the problem of discipline makes itself a small factor."
C. K.

The mathematics mistress reports:

"*From the Pupils' Standpoint.* In my opinion the pupil is the one who derives the greatest benefit from the Dalton Plan, and rightly so. If there was ever a time in the world's history when we needed people who could think and act independently, now is that time. Much of the failure in present-day politics is due to the fact that politicians are the slaves of other men's opinions. A pupil who works on the Dalton Plan cannot help doing his own thinking. He must rely upon his own resources, and surely that is what is expected of him in after life.

"Many people can do certain things well, but they fail lamentably when it comes to fitting those things into a larger scheme. It seems to me that the system of monthly assignments gives pupils a big outlook on their work. No matter how well they do one subject, the whole task is not satisfactory unless all the parts fit in. The completed task is like a large building which will collapse if one girder is weak. The children seem to realize that each subject must come up to a certain standard if their month's work is to be a success.

"From the Teacher's Standpoint. I feel sure that the average teacher would enjoy her work much more under the Dalton Plan than under the old class system. She can be free and at ease without losing her dignity. It is a great relief not to feel stilted and unnatural towards one's pupils. Now one feels like an older friend advising a younger one.

"Much of the failure of the old system was due to the fact that the teacher often found it impossible to locate the difficulties of the different pupils. A pupil cannot work even one day on the new plan before the teacher has found out some of his weaknesses. This simplifies her task.

"A really good teacher only tells her pupils what they cannot find out for themselves. We do not remember what we are told, but we do remember what we have to work hard to get." C. H. P.

After a year's experience of the Dalton Plan it was extended to the department of Art and Music, and though at first the teachers in these subjects had a good deal of difficulty in reorganizing their work on the new plan, they became as enthusiastic as their colleagues when its beneficial influence became apparent in better work and a finer spirit.

I give here the comments of these two instructors:

The art mistress says: "I like the atmosphere the Dalton Laboratory Plan creates in the laboratory. It is industrious, the children having come because of interest. It is thoughtful, the children intent on working out for themselves their problems through the assignments, asking help of the teacher only when a point needs further explanation. It is spontaneous, the children being able to get at the teacher when she is most needed at the particular time of their interest. It is quiet and orderly, inspiring one to work.

"Quite frankly, I am surprised to find how much I enjoy the Dalton Laboratory Plan. On the whole I now enjoy the laboratory period more than the class time. The class time is helpful in checking up the individuals as a class and so forth.

"I like the opportunity the Dalton Laboratory Plan gives for individual work. The teacher has more freedom so that she can help a child as long as seems necessary. The other children, having the assignment to work from, will not be losing time while she is thus occupied.

"The Dalton Laboratory Plan eliminates repeated directions, for the directions are all written out clearly in the assignment and the slower children can re-read them as many times as necessary for their understanding of the problem," H. T. B.

The music mistress states: "The Dalton Laboratory Plan strikes a new note in musical education. It gives an opportunity for individual expression which was not possible in class work.

"Often the child's apparent lack of musical appreciation is due to a command which he is not prepared to execute. As a result he acts through imitation. Under the Dalton Laboratory Plan his own experiments and experiences in music make him feel that music is a part of himself.

"Inaccuracies are more apparent and irritating in music than in other subjects. Only when difficulties are eliminated through individual work is a child's appreciation extended, or is he able to do his part in group work, *i.e.*, in the singing of part songs, in the orchestra, and so on.

"The Dalton Laboratory Plan permits the teacher to work with the children's undiluted interest. Personally I find that it gives me a feeling of great satisfaction. There is a thoroughness and a real progress without the interrupting and ruinous drill. The problems of discipline are eliminated and I find demonstrated in the attitude of the children as they work in the laboratory the real harmony for which one always aims." A. D.

In order to complete the picture I quote some opinions gathered from pupils of eight to twelve years. These children belonged to fourteen different nationalities, and their views given orally and taken down by a stenographer at the time were quite spontaneous.

QUESTION. "We have never discussed the plan of work used by the school since we began to use it. As I do not know how you feel about the plan I would appreciate your telling me whether you like it or not. I am asking for information."

L——, aged 12 years. "In this school a person that can't work as quickly as others in a particular subject takes that much more time for that subject and finishes all there is to be done. I like it for that reason. The record cards make each boy and girl do their work quicker because they can see just how much they have accomplished. They do the work better because they all want to finish their assignments, and the contract cards keep them in touch with each other's work. In other schools if you are sent into the mathematics room with your class you can't change and go into the English room when you're tired. But in our school, if you have been doing mathematics for some time you can change and go into some other room for a little while and then go back to mathematics if you want to. In other schools you have to work every minute, and if you try to stop to rest for a minute they make you go on. Here you can stop and rest and then get down to harder work again."

D——, aged 10 years. "If you are doing geography in other schools you take an awfully long time and don't finish, and then you have to go to mathematics, and you just sit there and waste time because you have done the mathematics already. In this school you can take the time saved on mathematics and put it with the geography time, and have enough time to get the geography finished right. If you study home work at night you are tired in school, and if you are made to work you don't do it well. Here, if you are too tired to work, you just sit still and read, and then pretty soon you feel like doing it. You never do things well that you are made to do.''

H——, aged 9 years. ''When you don't get a certain amount of work done in other schools you have to take it home and study it, and that makes you awfully tired. Here you just go on with it the next day. After a hard day's work at school you don't feel like studying at home. I like the plan because each one has ample time to do his work in, and if you get tired of doing one thing you can do another thing. I like the work better than I do in other schools. My main reason is that when you are absent you can begin to make up your work the next day. In other schools they may give you 50 minutes to do work, and it doesn't take you all that time, or sometimes they give you too little. You have to have just enough time to be suitable.''

G——, aged 10 years. ''I like the plan because we can go on and do our work and not be held back by children who are slower, and also because we can work hard and get through quickly, and get credit for the work we do well.''

W——, aged 11 years. ''In some schools when

you go into arithmetic you have to do arithmetic for half an hour, and you have to do so much that you get mixed up. Here, when you begin to get tired and can't make your mind work right on one thing, you can go into another room and forget all about the first thing, so you don't get muddled up. Later, you can do the first thing.''

A——, aged 9 years. ''At the end of the month, if you do your work very well, you are rewarded by your own satisfaction, and besides that, you may be put in a higher class.''

QUESTION. ''Wouldn't you like to have some other reward given to you—a medal or a book or something you very much wanted?''

ANSWER. ''No, that's not necessary, the satisfaction is enough. I'd rather just go ahead.''

QUESTION. ''At the beginning of the year I don't think you liked the plan at all, and you did not do as good work. What was the trouble?''

(This question was unfair, but it was given as a challenge.)

V——, aged 9 years. ''We were so glad to get into a school where we could be let alone for a little while that we took a vacation.''

E——, aged 9 years. ''At the beginning of the year everybody was thinking more about other things than about the work.''

P——, aged 10 years. ''We did not understand how to work.''

G——, aged 9 years. ''In the beginning, we were still a little shy because we did not know the teachers and what they expected of us. We hadn't been used to the way of working here, and we had been used to all taking the same subject at once, and then we didn't get the same attention.''

J——, aged 9 years. "At the beginning they were used to another way, and it took them some time to understand."

QUESTION. "Do you feel you need a recess in the morning?" (We call a "break" a recess.) They all said "No." One boy, aged 10 years, explained, "No, we take a recess ourselves when we are tired. We can sit down and read."

QUESTION. "You have told all the nice things, what about the faults of the plan?" The children said they had no fault to find with it. This was unanimous.

One boy was appointed by the other children to come to me afterwards. I was at tea with a small group of people when the child came in. He said: "I beg your pardon, may I speak to you?" My reply was: "Certainly, what is it?" He said, quietly: "It is something private. May we step into the next room?" I went immediately. Then he proceeded: "I don't want to be rude, Miss Parkhurst, but the children think you do not like the plan. They like it very much, and they have sent me to ask you why you don't like it? Aren't you going to get behind it?" (He meant "support it.")

I assured him that I was interested and would,

to the best of my ability, "get behind the plan." I
sincerely appreciated the interest shown in their
challenge. It became, from that moment, more
than ever THEIR plan, and I was helped to a better
perspective.

The children in this school have no "home
work," though they are supplied with cultural
reading lists as a guide for filling unoccupied time.
Some of the boys entered the school with very
poor records, one or two having been in four different schools in as many years. When their
energy was harnessed by the Dalton Plan to a real
job, the majority gave an excellent account of
themselves, and even the slowest child got through
his year's assignment. The staff agree that the
children have become more simple, straightfor-
ward, and enthusiastic, and free from emotional
conflicts. The nervous mannerisms with which a
few were afflicted have disappeared. As a body
they are mature, but not in the least sophisticated.
They have, in a word, found themselves.

In conclusion, there is one point which I want to
emphasize. The Dalton Laboratory Plan must
not be regarded as a cast-iron scheme. I offer it
as a first step towards the evolution of a scheme of
education which will develop the creative faculty
in both teachers and pupils. I have been animated
in elaborating it by a desire to remedy some of the
ills our schools are heirs to, and especially the
worst of these, which is, I believe, the absence of
opportunity for the learner to learn. Teachers

go to training colleges to acquire the art of teaching before they practise it, so pupils should be given the chance to acquire the art of study before they can be expected to learn. I am content that the Dalton Plan, which I have not even sought to brand with my name, should be judged by its fruits. Those fruits have already, on the testimony of numerous teachers and pupils, changed for the better the mental and spiritual life of the schools to which the plan has been applied. This testimony gives me faith that the benefits there reaped will be ultimately carried into the social and politic life of the world. I do not claim to have perfected my plan. Many minds must concentrate and co-operate upon it if it is to be a living and vital thing. If it stimulates sufficient interest to attract the finest energies of the educational profession to the task, I shall be amply rewarded for my part of the great work.

CHAPTER IX

A Year's Experiment in an English Secondary School[*]

By Rosa Bassett, M.B.E., M.A., Head Mistress Streatham County Secondary School

The article in the *Times Educational Supplement* of May 27th, 1920, set many people thinking. The Dalton Plan seemed so simple in its conception, so far-reaching in its possibilities, that one wondered why it had never been thought of before.

We, although a large school now of over 700 girls, decided to try the experiment as soon as we could. Thanks to the broad views of the Board of Education and of the London County Council we have been able to test it for over a year, with the result that we feel it enlists, more than any other plan does, the co-operation of the pupil in her education. It has undoubtedly made her study more than before, though its effects may not be at once apparent, for naturally the ordinary testing devices cannot gauge the growth of the child's understanding. We are, in fact, but slowly finding out how to test intelligence.

[*] Reprinted by kind permission of the *Times*.

The plan seems quite simple in America because there pupils in a High School rarely carry more than six major subjects. In an English school most students carry nine or ten, but the plan is carried out better in an English Public School because we have more freedom here. It is carried out better, too, in an English school because the teachers are better trained and better qualified and have more freedom and leisure than in an American High School. Of course, the plan succeeds only when the staff is capable and keen as well as qualified and trained. It is due to the hearty co-operation of the staff here that we have been able to undertake it at all.

At the beginning of each month every girl receives a syllabus of work to be done in each subject. One lesson at least is given in each subject during the week, the subject matter to be taken in these lessons being usually indicated in the syllabus.

The whole of Tuesday morning and part of three afternoons are devoted to class lessons. There is a fixed time-table for these occasions. In addition to this, the third forms have lessons on Thursday morning: thus the greater part of the school have all Monday, Wednesday, and Thursday mornings for free study. There is group work on Friday mornings. Each mistress announces beforehand the topics to be dealt with; she may perhaps summon some individuals to attend, but in the main attendance is voluntary.

Subjects are, as far as possible, studied in subject rooms, where the subject mistress may be consulted. Each girl is expected to see the mistress at least once a week on an average, apart from set lessons. She may, of course, stay the whole session in one room if she wishes. The mistress is always there to advise her, or to correct her work. There are subject libraries in the subject rooms.

Every girl must be present at the set lessons, but apart from this she may arrange her working time at school and at home as she pleases. Her free time at school is 34 periods of 40 minutes each, minus set lesson periods; her home work periods should not be more than from 5 to 15 in a week, according to her position in the school. She is responsible for giving the right proportion of time during the month to all the subjects in her curriculum, and she indicates on the charts in the subject rooms the time she has given and the amount of work she has done.

A girl must satisfy the subject mistress before she begins the next syllabus. This may be established by test, or by any method that the mistress finds most suitable for the girl.

Assignments.

Assignments are given in three parts in each subject.

1. *Lower.* This should be within the range of the slowest girl in the class, and must be done by all.

2. *Middle.* Gives opportunity for wider reading and deeper thought.

3. *Higher.* Encourages the brilliant girl to study as far as she can go.

Middle and Higher pupils do not encroach on the next month's assignment. Girls choose grades for themselves; sometimes the weakest have to be advised not to attempt too much.

APPORTIONMENT OF PERIODS (subjects and forms).

The first column gives *total* periods that should be spent weekly (lessons and study at home and in school). The second column gives number of class lessons. Optional subjects are shown by an asterisk.

Forms:

	Total Lessons.		Total Lessons.		Total Lessons.		Total Lessons.		Total Lessons.	
Scripture........	1	1	1	1	1	1	1	1	1	1
English..........	5	2	6	2	6	2	6	2	6	1
History..........	3	1	6	2						
Geography.......	3	1			6	2	6	2	6	1
French..........	6	4	6	3	6	2	6	2	6	1
2nd Foreign Language......					6	3*	6	2*	6	2
Arithmetic.......	6	2					3	1		
Mathematics.....	2	1	6	3	6	2	6	2*	6	2
Science..........	3	2	6	2	6	2	6	2	6	2
Drawing.........	3	1	3	1	3	1	3	1	1	1
Needlework......	3	1	3	1	3	1	3	1	3	plus 2*
								or		
Cooking.........					3	1	3	1		
Singing..........	2	2	1	1	1	1	1	1	1	1
Gym. and Games	3	3	2	2	2	2	2	2	2	2

History and geography are taken in alternate years by the third and fourth forms, and for half the year each in the lower fifth form. In the upper fifth pupils may take either subject, or both.

A teacher does not necessarily give a lesson in the class lesson period. She may merely give an explanation or direction and allow the class to study during the rest of the period.

Ideally, all work should be carried on in the subject rooms; in reality, with us, a certain amount of work has to be carried on in the Hall. Although every mistress has outside her door a table showing on what days, or parts of days, the room is open to certain forms or open to all, it sometimes happens that a child starts out with books for two or three subjects in her arms and finds each of those subject rooms crowded. In that case she has to work in the Hall. Both in subject rooms and in the Hall girls are allowed to work quietly together. This is another reason for the gradual lessening of subject antipathies.

Our School "Parliament" voices from time to time protests against overcrowded rooms and the selfishness of individuals who borrow reference books from the libraries and leave them at home.

We have learnt much from the children. We occasionally invite their comments, and when we do these are candidly and generously given. We have frequently followed the children's suggestions and amended our plans to the advantage of both school and staff.

The following is a typical set of questions given to the school at the end of the first year of work under the Dalton Plan:

1. Does this system alter your outlook in regard to books and reading?
2. In which subject or subjects have you improved?
3. In which subject do you consider you have not gained?
4. Do you agree with girls working together? Does it benefit them?
5. What are the advantages of this system?
6. How would you improve it?
7. What are the disadvantages?

The answers were scribbled down rapidly by the pupils gathered together for the purpose in the school hall, and were handed in anonymously, marked only with the pupils' age, before the meeting dispersed. There are over 700 girls in the school, but we need consider only six answers which, by their frankness or *naïveté,* throw light on the spontaneous reaction of the pupils to their environment.

1. "It has made me more fond of books, and it has improved my reading. It has also taught me to express myself better in essays."
    "Books interest me more now, for one thing, if I get through my syllabus quickly I have more time to read."
    "I think that this has made me read more

books, because I look up things and then read the whole book.''

"I prefer the widened library. Reading has helped me a lot. I like the new and more interesting books we now have in the library (*e.g.*, New Liberty) better than old books of plain facts, etc.''

"Under the old scheme I should have depended on hearing what a mistress would tell me and looked up any books; now I look up as many books as possible.''

"I take more interest in the books I am reading now because there is a variety, and we do not now have just to read from one or two books during the term. For History, instead of the whole class getting the same idea on a subject, everyone tackles the subject from a different point of view.''

2. The majority of girls seem to think they have improved in History, Geography, and English, a good many state that their Mathematics and Science are both better under this system.

3. In Modern Languages girls feel that their pronunciation may have suffered. The type of girl who complains that she has to rely on her own brains now instead of on the mistress' thinks that many subjects suffer.

4. In the answers to this question opinion is divided. There is no doubt girls like working together if they are fairly even, and a weak girl likes to have help from a stronger one, but many state that the weak rely too much upon the strong.

"In most cases I think the strong girl does

the work while the weak girl thinks she understands and takes it for her own. She would learn more if she worked alone.''

''Girls have a chance to help one another . . . what some girls don't know, others do know.''

''We learn more, for now we have our own thoughts and another girl's thoughts.''

''It enables you to be more friendly towards one another.''

''Girls have become, on the whole, more kindly disposed to one another, not so many cliques are formed; more co-operation.''

''The strong girl gets time to help the weak.''

5. ''Girls who work quickly are not held back by the slower girls.''

''Those girls who are quicker can get on in front of others without waiting for them.''

''If a girl is behind in a subject the form does not wait for the girl, but goes on.''

''The better girls do not have to wait for the slower ones to catch up, and hear the same things explained many times when they understand it.''

''I have more time and get more work done.''

''I need never pass over a thing which I do not understand.''

''Those girls who are not so quick can get help from the mistresses, and so get along quicker than they did before.''

''The slower girls can ask help many times without feeling the class is going too quickly for them.''

"You can take as long as you like on a subject."

"You do not have to do a thing at once, you can think it over and leave it for another day."

"The advantages cover a wide field. Apart from the wider reading, girls appreciate the advantage to the individual and the benefit to the work itself."

"There is no need to keep changing the subject."

"When the bell rings you do not have to leave off in the middle of a piece of work and be obliged to go on to another lesson."

"Under the old system we often had to break off in the middle of something on Monday and wait until Wednesday to finish it."

"You learn to be absorbed in your work."

And the natural corollary follows:

"We learn to work more thoroughly and not to be slack as sometimes you can be in class."

"I can get more work done in school and much less at home."

"The knowledge gained is not so stodgy."

"We learn to work properly and diligently, and it is not so dull as having a dry lesson."

Many girls note a change in the moral atmosphere of the school, and the setting in of a far more fundamental discipline:

"There is much more responsibility for us in this system."

"When I am not under a mistress's eye I

think I can work better, because it gives me an idea that I am trusted to work, and so I do.''

"It helps you to learn to be quiet when a mistress is not there to keep you quiet."

"The advantages of this system are that it makes girls feel that they are reliable."

"We learn what the word 'trust' means."

Others note the tonic effect of the system upon themselves:

"You learn to think for yourself, and not to depend on a mistress."

"The system helps you not to lean on a mistress."

"It teaches you how to teach yourself."

"I used to rely on the mistresses and do scarcely any reading, but now I rely on them less and read much more."

"I have studied more books than I should have done under the old scheme, when I should have depended on hearing what mistresses would tell me, and should not have looked up any books; now I look up as many books as possible."

"I have found often under the old scheme that I cannot work out a sum or a theorem or write an essay from sheer tiredness of the subject. It is at these times you feel how much more pleasant your own time-table would be."

6. One poor child who evidently dislikes both work and responsibility would improve the plan by abolishing the whole thing:

"I would do away with the whole system. Nearly all of it. Why should we as Britons copy Americans, why not use ideas of our own? Our temperament is not suited to so much work, as we have not been brought up to it from childhood, as have the Americans."

Many would improve by abolishing tests or giving different kind of test:

"For instance, in History I should prefer a question such as, 'Say all you can about the Indian Mutiny, its causes, the results on India, and on government in England and India."

"In History we had, 'How was the colonization of Australia a result of the revolt of Canada?' For the growth of the British Empire I had taken each part separately, and learnt how they became parts of the British Empire. I did not make any relation between them. If the question had been, 'How did certain parts of the British Empire come under British rule?' I could have answered that better, and would have shown that I knew more about the growth of the British Empire than the former question would lead one to believe."

Others would have periods for silent work; many ask for more books and for less crowded rooms.

7. The disadvantages given are often at opposite points of the compass. Some would have more lessons, some would have fewer:

"It takes longer to gather from books that which can be gathered from mistresses."

"One of the disadvantages is that a girl is tempted to leave the subjects she dislikes and to work only at those she is fond of. This was avoided when we had to attend three or four lessons in a subject in a week."

"For girls who cannot concentrate it is far more difficult to get information from a book than from someone who can make the subject interesting and give information away from the dry facts."

"In learning from books many people cannot pick out the most important facts, but make twice as much work by learning trivial points of no real value."

It would be folly to imagine that even so fine a conception as the Dalton Plan finds in any English school universal and welcome acceptance, either from staff or scholars. The more conservative teachers naturally, at first, look askance at an untried scheme, fearing that their authority will be set at naught and their years of accumulated knowledge and facility in teaching will become of little value. But no scheme would be worth consideration if it did not recognize that the teacher cannot abrogate her authority and responsibility, and must not waste her experience and knowledge. The Dalton Plan creates so intimate a bond between pupil and teacher that the latter becomes less of an autocrat and more of a guide. Our stores of knowledge are open to all who wish to enter. "If thou seest a man of understanding get thee betimes unto him, and let thy foot near the steps of his door," said the writer of Ecclesiasticus. With more freedom in the school this becomes possible now.

Young, untrained teachers are, moreover, often unable to grasp, in all its bearings, a change so new to their experience. Their sole stock-in-trade is their university career and their remembrance of how they were taught at school. The lymphatic teacher again is apt to sit down under the scheme. She, the pupils, and the plan are three points with no connection, and she sometimes needs more supervision than do the pupils, for the feeble, uninspired teacher produces followers equally feeble and uninspired. But the person with faith, experience, who possesses knowledge of, and love for, the child, brings forth fruit a hundredfold. The delight of the Dalton Plan lies in the fact that it is capable of many interpretations and extensions. The principles of freedom and initiative belong to the director as well as to the pupil.

On the whole, it is these people who have seen little or nothing of the workings of the plan who are most fertile in criticism which may range from strain on pupils and staff to the size of desks that fit the varying occupants, or to the length of a vertical line in marking a graph. The question of strain on pupils falls under two heads: eye strain and nerve strain. There are those who fear that pupils will suffer from reading during too long a period. But in reality this rarely happens, for normal boys and girls do not work to fatigue point; they stop reading in order to discuss, or they change their subject.

The question of worrying about work and over responsibility is, however, a serious consideration in any school; if teachers are not alive to the importance of the all-round development, physical as well as mental and moral, of their pupils, this can arise in any system. But under the Dalton Plan, where the teacher is so much more closely in touch with the pupil, the possibility of worrying over responsibility is lessened. The child who shudders at responsibility is just the person who needs a sympathetic initiation into self-reliance. Under a *sympathetic teacher* she gets this opportunity. Each child is considered as an individual; her work and its results are shaped to her needs. Under any system the heedless child who neglects her work may get worried and flustered at the end of the term. Now we find fewer who neglect their work and fewer who are worried over it.

Any plan at its initiation entails more thought and more conferences on the part of the staff. Thought runs in a new direction. No longer does one think how to bring the matter, the information, to the child, but how to lead the child to find it out for himself. One thinks how to arouse and maintain that interest in dealing with a subject, so that work becomes a "breath and finer spirit." Naturally, when after much effort the early sylla-

buses showed inperfections, and pupils did not do
what they expected to do, a little feeling of disap-
pointment may have made one feel that the work
was heavier than before. But as months went on,
efforts and thought produced so much more remunerative work from pupils that this strain was
lessened. Some people seem to think that in the
laboratory periods teachers sit and watch children
work; others picture a queue of pupils each asking
the same question, and the teacher wearied out
with giving the same reply. But the truth is that
the teacher *lives,* still has common sense, still
guides and suggests, amends and reforms plans of
earlier days.

Maybe the super-specialist laments the possible
disappearance of the inspirational lecture. When
one remembers speeches and sermons and lessons
that were a joy and an inspiration, one realizes
how much the value depended upon the stirring of
the emotions, and how that value was increased by
discussion or reading afterwards. The influence
of a teacher upon her class is not at its greatest
height during a lesson no matter how inspirational the lesson may be. The brilliant child ad-
mires the fine lesson and values the teacher for
that. The average child is moved by it; the
slower child may be awed by it. But for actual
remunerative effort a few words spoken to a be-
wildered child, putting her at ease with her difficulty, and giving her guidance for the future,
may be more potent than the finest class lesson. It

is doubtful whether any teacher could give more than one really inspiring lesson a week to every form. We may give several lessons weekly that satisfy us; they do not necessarily inspire the class. Under the Dalton Plan the lesson that inspires still has its place, particularly when a new subject, or a new stage of a subject, or a great topic is in consideration. The following up of the forces set in motion by such a lesson is now possible with individual work.

There are still others who have a vision of a jaded staff burning the midnight oil over corrections. The group work should tend to lessen the amount to be corrected. Group discussion and inter-group discussion may well take the part of the written exercise. What is important for every teacher to remember is that freshness and vigour, both of mind and body, are more advantageous to the pupil than a series of thoroughly corrected exercises which rarely repay the time so spent even if they are things that *can be displayed* when occasion arises.

The proportion of set lessons to free study period varies according to the needs of a particular form or the needs of a particular subject at a particular time. The abolition of such lessons is not an essential part of the plan, and where the number of pupils to a teacher is large this is practically an impossibility.

Many critics of the Dalton Plan fear it may bring a lessening of form spirit, or corporate life.

If class lessons were the only essential in the growth of form spirit every class in every school in England would be a strong corporate body. When the atmosphere of the school and the spirit of the staff are good, corporate feeling will grow under any system. The consideration by the teacher of each child as an individual does not mean that children pass through school as separate units. Groups feel pride in group achievement, forms feel pride in form achievement, whether in work or in games. Corporate life is almost wholly a social development. Class lessons and mark sheets will not make a form a living body.

There is also a feeling that shirkers may lead a too happy life under the new plan. Of course, the teacher must keep this danger in mind. It can usually be arrested by suggesting better work to them, and when suggestion fails, she can keep them steadily at work by an individual time-table till they are fit to enjoy the liberty of the plan. But as one progresses in making syllabuses which must focus the child's view-point, interest becomes a great incentive and shirkers become few.

Another evil which specialists dread is that pupils will work too vigorously at their favourite subjects and shun their difficult ones. They fear, too, that pupils will flock to the room of the favourite teacher and avoid others. Naturally, the pupil tends to go where she is warmly welcomed, encouraged, and helped, and tends to avoid the person who greets her with a reproof. Where any feeling of animosity exists it will lessen the amount of joy and vigour and success in work. But if all specialist teachers interest themselves in the pupils' all-around progress more than in any special subject, no animosity will arise. All teachers should realize that children *want* to learn, and that every means of helping them to fulfil that want should be employed, even at the price of ceasing to be censorious and of becoming a guide and a friend. The real discipline which a child develops by joyously and steadily pursuing a course is far better for her character than the feeling of shame or resentment aroused by reproof, even though resentment were followed by good work. The curious thing is that when children have a choice of subject and of time, and when they begin to exercise judgment, they discriminate between the popular teacher and the teacher who helps. To their credit, be it said, they go where knowledge is. It is well for a child to have an absorbing interest in a subject, and if one appreciates this at its proper worth, interest spreads from one to the other subjects. Even if it were not so, it would still be better for a child to leave school with this one interest than with a carefully calculated and evenly spread amount of general information. The class advisor and the pupil's graph card help to keep a fairly all-round state of progress though, of course, some will always work the minimum at certain subjects and the highest in others.

Accuracy and neatness are the next points assailed. Any good teacher knows where accuracy is *essential,* where neatness is *essential,* and will not let the child ruin otherwise good efforts by failure in these directions. Children appreciate tests for accuracy; they see their worth. They like to give up a neatly-written paper well-expressed and well-spelt, though their rough notes may be abominable. A child gives full expression to her ideas in discussion or in writing rough notes, but ideas can often be hampered by too great insistence upon writing and neatness.

Oral work and speech training loom largely in the eyes of other critics. In class work the articulate pupils speak during most of the time while the inarticulate listen, or dream, or stammer forth a few words. Their ideas have no flow because they are so conscious of the criticism of their fellows and of their teachers that they are loath to take up the time of the class. Under the Dalton Plan a self-conscious child has a greater chance. She is in closer contact with the teacher; she realizes that she is not taking up the time of the class in her efforts to express herself. Moreover, when dealing with her as an individual, the teacher can find some point of interest, perhaps very remotely connected with the subject in hand, but one capable of unlocking the child's mind and of enabling her to give expression freely to something which interests her. When once aroused in this way, a child grows more and more awake to other points of view and becomes no longer the tongue-tied laggard of the class. Correction of speech defects is received in a far more kindly spirit when the child is by the teacher's side, and possibilities for correction are more frequent. Now oral composition has become a valuable exercise.

While admitting that the plan may be successful with the brilliant child, who, in the eyes of the critic, will take most of the teacher's time, doubts are often expressed, that it would be less successful with the slower child. One must confess that the brilliant child progresses at a far greater rate than before, but, at the same time, one must also acknowledge that the slower child progresses, too, at a greater rate and in a far better way. The very slow child always needs special consideration, and is able to get it either as an individual or in a group. The fear that exists in some minds with regard to the last type is that such pupils will not really enjoy prolonged periods of private study. First of all, I must point out that the pupil is not obliged to study for prolonged periods. She may change her subject as she will. Moreover, she *does* enjoy discussion of her study with her teacher or with other girls. Probably she would not enjoy a week of all study with no lessons or no manual work or drill or games. But freedom to do some amount of the work by herself certainly brings with it increased enjoyment of the work undertaken.

Another critic asks: "What is the moral effect of allowing children to choose their occupation at certain times when, in after life, they will have to do what is set before them at a given time?" If a rigid time-table of class lessons had produced a nation whose ideals were so high that everything was done from a sense of duty and discipline—a nation so developed that self-discipline was universal, one would be disinclined to contemplate any change in educational methods. But as no such nation exists, one is justified in hoping that a change may be for the better, and that an education based upon freedom to choose, and to pursue the study that attracts where and when the student wills may assist us to grow into a nation competent to choose and pursue its own destiny rather than one led by the voice of authority whether in the form of a ranting demagogue, a trumpery journal, a fashion plate, or a phrase. In the world people "do what is set before them at a given time" either because it is to their interest, or because it is their livelihood. Children who grow up with a joy in the work which interests them will be likely to find that interest useful in their later life. It is certain at all events, that our education which allows a child liberty to develop and time to think and plan must favour the expansion of all the good qualities innate in his personality.

CHAPTER X

THE DALTON PLAN FOR ELEMENTARY SCHOOLS

By JOHN EADES, Head Master of Kirkstall Road Council
School, Leeds

THE DALTON PLAN has come to stay. It has already secured its place in the secondary school, and has also been adopted in many elementary schools. In fact, in various modified forms it had been in use in some English up-to-date schools long before it came from America. I hope to give such information of the initiation and working of the new plan in the elementary school as will enable any teachers who are interested to apply the plan to suit their own school and their own particular circumstances.

A number of years ago I began a system of specialization at the Leeds Kirkstall Road School. The frequent hearing of class lessons on all the school subjects prepared and given by students in training convinced me of the impossibility of any one teacher being able to do full justice to every subject in the curriculum. Tastes, training, disposition, and knowledge were all against it. It was self-evident that a teacher always taught those subjects best that he knew most about, and they were invariably the subjects in which he was most interested. All teachers have one or more such subjects, and their enthusiasm and keenness with regard to them often inspire their pupils, and so secure more and better work with a much less expenditure of energy.

We discussed the question at several staff meetings, and talked over the preferences of the various teachers. Then two or more special subjects were allotted to each teacher; the time-table was arranged accordingly, and ever since specialization in teaching has been used in our school with gratifying success.

Yet as time went on, the weakness and waste of cumulative class teaching in some subjects became painfully manifest. Listening to hundreds of lessons in academic subjects—carefully and often elaborately prepared—and seeing the utterly inadequate result of it all, turned my mind in the direction of sectional teaching. Classes were divided into three sections—one containing the clever children, the middle one the average children, and the third section the weaker and backward children. This was an improvement on whole class teaching, yet it left something to be desired, and we were still faced by the problem of the individual—the problem that each child in our charge is *unique;* for no two children in the world are exactly alike, each one has a personality distinct from that of anybody else. Every time a child exercises his will, the action has a separate and direct effect upon the formation of his character, which as time goes on makes him a distinct unit, requiring distinct and separate treatment; for we can deal with these personalities successfully only by treating them individually, and applying our methods according to the disposition and capacity of each child.

Some three or four years ago this thought led to individual work being given to those in the seventh standard, the children being allotted one week's work at a time. Then the Dalton Plan arrived, and that led to further developments. But before going into detail let me summarize some of the disadvantages of the class teaching of academic subjects which urged us to adopt a different plan.

Sharp children are held back and dull children are pushed on, to the detriment of their mental powers, owing to the teacher's effort to strike the problematical average.

Lazy children do as little as they can, and shelter themselves behind the more eager ones.

There is very little in the way of co-operation, and co-operation is one of the vital principles of successful teaching. The teacher is tempted to pour into the minds of the children a load of new facts, and his teaching resolves itself into "talk a little, chalk a little, talk a little more"; while the children remain passive, and often become indifferent and mischievous. Any lesson, to be effective, must be the children's as well as the teacher's, and more the children's than the teacher's.

Then again, a child has to take stated subjects, each at a definite time, for a given length of time, whether he feels in the humour for a particular subject or no. And the one who finds a subject difficult can spend only the same amount of time at it as the one who finds it easy. This arrangement generates in the child a distaste for that subject; whereas if he had more time to spend on it and more help given to him, he would overcome his difficulties and find real interest in the very work which once he disliked. And, finally, more rapid promotion is a serious problem under the ordinary method of classification. The only way seems to be for a clever child to spend six months in one standard and then pass on to the next. But this means a serious gap in a scheme of work and breaks the thread of the child's orderly and graduated education, which, in the long run, probably does more harm than good.

To avoid these disadvantages, some subjects should be taught individually and others in groups or classes.

All teaching can be broadly divided into two sections: (1) That which aims at the development of the mental powers, and the acquirement of such knowledge as is necessary to make an intelligent and useful citizen; and (2) that which has for its object the development of the physique, the cultivation of the social sense, and of the emotions.

With these two aims in mind, we can, broadly speaking, divide our school subjects into two groups corresponding in the main to these two aims:

1. The academic subjects—*e.g.*, reading, mathematics, physical science, composition, spelling, grammar, history, geography, art and handicraft corresponding to our first aim.

2. The physical, social, and emotional subjects —*e.g.*, physical training (including games and dancing), music, literature, outdoor rambles, for nature study and sketching, and lantern lectures, corresponding to our second aim. There will be some overlapping in (1) and (2), but nothing detrimental to the plan.

The academic subjects will be taught individually, and sometimes in small groups where children are at the same stage. There will be individual co-operation—the younger ones will be encouraged to seek help from the older ones, and the older ones will be encouraged to give it.

The other subjects will be taught in classes, but the classification will be mainly an age classification and not one of standards. In these lessons there will be communal co-operation; and it is only by a happy use of both kinds of co-operation that the best social life and the finest character can be attained.

The first thing to do is to decide on the standards to be brought within the scheme; ours are standards IV to VIII. When that is done, arrange the classrooms for the various subjects according to the work allotted to the different members of the staff. Our rooms are arranged and labelled as follows:

The Hall—Reading.

Room 1—Art.

Room 2—History and Geography.

Room 3—English (composition, spelling, and grammar).

Room 4—Mathematics.

Room 5—Science and Handicraft.

The teacher who has specialized in the subjects named takes charge of his room and the work that has to be done in it. I take charge of the reading, which is, of course, silent reading, and that brings me into close and frequent contact with every pupil in the upper part of the school.

A monthly allotment of work in each subject is made out by the teacher responsible and fixed on the classroom wall or notice board. It does not exceed an amount which can be done comfortably by a child of ordinary ability. Children are allowed to copy this into their notebooks either as a whole or in parts as they require them.

At 9.30 a.m. the gong is sounded, the scripture lesson closes, the children move out into any room they prefer, and stay there as long as they like; so there may be, and there usually are, children from all the given standards in any one room at the same time. Some stay for half an hour, others for an hour, and a few for a whole morning. Each pupil plans out his own work, and does it at his own convenience. No slacking is allowed. A boy

WORK RECORD CARD		
Std 6 James Edge		
Subject	May	June
Arith	S.12... W.1x0456.	S.1255... W.12565
Geom	1255	12
Science	1.2	1.2
Comp	1234 H85	123 H85
Gram	S.1 W. 85s.	S.1 85s
Spell	S. 85s.	S. W 85s
Geog.	S.1.5 W.12545	S.45 W.1.25.45
History	S.12565 W.25660	S.1255 W.12365
Read.	S.1 9/2 W.1.2	S.1 9/2 W.1.2
Art.	1. L.M.P.	2. O.P.

S = SET WORK. W = WRITTEN WORK.

must be reading, studying, writing, drawing, modelling, experimenting, etc. The teacher questions each one briefly on his study work, discusses

points with him, and examines his written answers
to the questions set.

Each child is supplied with a "Work Record
Card." This he keeps in an envelope in his school
bag, along with his writing materials and text-
books, for the preservation and safety of which he
is held responsible.

When the teacher has questioned a boy on any
part of his set work, or has corrected one of his
written answers, he marks it with a tick in red
ink. All the teacher's marks on the card are in
red ink; my initials, as the head master, when the
work for the month is completed, are in black ink.

When the teacher has initialled his monthly
allotment as being completed, he ticks off the boy's
name for that month in his own book, which contains the names of all the boys in their various
standards. When I have initialled the completed
month's work, I enter in my book, opposite the
name of each boy, a number corresponding to the
order of finishing among the boys of the same
standard. In this way we can find out at any
time just where a boy stands in his work, and a
request for his record card will furnish the details.

No boy is allowed to go on with any subject
in one month's allotment until he has completed
the work given in all the subjects set for the previous month. Many children will have the March
work finished in February, and the April work
finished in early March. Then if they prefer they
can spend the remaining time in the month on

their favourite subjects—and probably they will
be better educated through these than through
any others—or they can push on with the next
month's allotment. Most children prefer to do
the latter, and many will complete the year's work
in seven, eight, or nine months, and at once pass
on to the work of the next standard higher. The
slower ones may take 15 or 16 months to do the
year's work; but when they have done it, it will
be well done, and will do them far more good
than merely skimming the work in their efforts to
keep pace with those who are more mentally alert.

Oral lessons are not barred during the working
of the Dalton Plan. The personal, individual intercourse between teacher and pupils enables the
teacher to find out their peculiar difficulties. If
the same difficulty presents itself to several children the teacher makes a note of it, and gathers
them round the blackboard, and deals with their
difficulty there.

In other parts of a subject set for study it may
not be possible for the children to obtain all the
necessary information from their text-books, or
the reference books which are provided, and to
which children are frequently sent for further
information. When that happens, perhaps once
or twice a month, the teacher appoints a day and
time, and puts up a notice, or enters it on the
allotment of work, asking all children who are
studying that subject to assemble in his room for
a special lesson. Other children in the room at

the time go to one of the other subject-rooms, and carry on work there.

Here are a few of our specimen allotments of work for a month:

STANDARD IV

HISTORY

March

STUDY.

(*a*) How a monastery got its food and money.
(*b*) The Friars.
(*c*) A mediaeval town in the time of Edward III (14th century).
[See *Piers' Plowman History*, pp. 118-139.]

WRITTEN WORK.

(*a*) Make a sketch of the stocks on page 134, but leave out the drawings of the man and woman.
(*b*) Give an account of the Friars in your own words.
(*c*) What do you think the streets of Leeds were like in the 14th century?
(*d*) Tell what you know of the trade guilds.

ENGLISH

February

COMPOSITION.

Select any four of the following subjects; collect and arrange ideas on each of them, and then write compositions on them in your books.

(*a*) A rainy day.
(*b*) My mother, or father.
(*c*) A description of a favourite toy.
(*d*) A letter to a chum telling him what fun you had in making a snow man.
(*e*) An accident on the ice.
Give two accounts of this:
(1) By the injured person.
(2) By one of those who went to his aid.

GRAMMAR.

Study pages 13 and 14 in your English books. Write out exercise 10, and underline the *pronouns*.

SPELLING.

Write out the transcription exercise on pages 44 and 45. Learn the words printed in thick black type, and be prepared to use them in oral sentences.

SPECIAL LESSON.

On Monday, February 6th, at 9.30, a lesson will be given on "Punctuation." All Standard IV boys must be present; any others who know that their punctuation is faulty may also attend.

STANDARD V

GEOMETRY

March

(1) Draw an equilateral triangle of 3 inches side. Divide this triangle into three equal tri-

angles. In each triangle inscribe a circle which will just touch all the sides.

(2) On a given base line, say 2 inches, show the method of erecting any polygon.

(3) Draw the plan, elevation, and end elevation of the following hand sketch of a model.

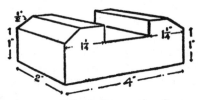

(4) Select any object from the box of models, and draw the plan, elevation, and end elevation of it to a scale half the size.

ARITHMETIC

March

STUDY.

(1) Study the multiplication and division of decimals on pages 32 and 33 of the Cambridge Arithmetic.

(2) Draw Figure 1, on page 35, and do what it tells you at the side.

(3) Read No. 4 on page 36, and work an example of your own on squared paper.

(4) Complete the table about prices at the top of page 39.

(5) Learn the meaning of Ratio from the example at the top of page 43, and study both the unitary method and the fractional method.

WRITTEN WORK.

Work examples:
(1) (*a*), (*b*), (*c*) in No. 10, p. 32.
(2) (5), (6), (9) on p. 33.
(3) (3), (4), (5), (6) on p. 37.
(4) (1), (2), (3) on p. 40.
(5) (5), (6), (7) on p. 46.

SPECIAL LESSON.

On Friday morning, March 10th, at 9.30, a lesson on ''The Uses of Ratio'' will be given to all boys in Standard V who are at this stage of the work. Other boys may attend if they wish to do so.

STANDARD VI

ART

March

Do the work indicated in any four of the following sections:

OBJECT DRAWING.

Make a water-colour drawing of the group of objects set up for March in your section of the room.

MEMORY DRAWING.

Draw from memory a group of objects comprising a jackplane, a dovetail saw, a mallet and a chisel. When you are in the Handicraft Department notice carefully the construction and shape of these tools.

DESIGN.

Draw two border designs, one based on straight lines and one on curved lines. Paint them, using those colours which, in your opinion, harmonize the best.

LETTERING.

Study the examples of Roman lettering which are displayed. The proportions of the letters up to K are shown. Draw these carefully, making your squares of 2 inches sides. Notice that certain letters, such as C, D, G, are based on the circle.

PICTURE DRAWING.

Watch boys or men playing football. Notice the positions of arms and legs when one is taking a big kick. Make drawings of a footballer kicking the football from different positions. Illustrate an incident in a football match which may be entitled "Saved!"

GEOGRAPHY

February

STUDY.

Study the products and industries of India, and then the towns and communications.

Read Lay's *British Dominions,* pp. 50–63. Seek further information in the reference books.

WRITTEN WORK.

(1) In map reading and exercises, do numbers 4, 9, 12, 13 on p. 54, and 3, 15, 17 on p. 61.

(2) In "Things to do" take numbers 1, 2 on p. 55, and 1, 2 on p. 62.

SPECIAL LESSON.

A lesson will be given on Monday, February 27th, at 11 a.m., on "The Value of India to Britain and the Value of Britain to India." All boys who are studying India must be present.

READING

April

When you have chosen your book for the month, enter your name, standard, and title of the book in the exercise book provided for the purpose.

Read through the whole of the book before you write any answers.

If, in reading, you come to anything you do not understand, ask one of the older boys or consult the dictionary. If these do not help you, come to me.

When you have read through the book give written answers to the following questions:

(1) Which do you consider the best story or the most interesting chapter in the book? Describe it.

(2) Which person in the book do you like best? Say why you prefer him (or her), and tell of one or two things he did.

(3) Write a short play, using the contents of any chapter in the book, or write a poem of not less than three verses about any person or incident in the book.

STANDARD VII

ENGLISH

March

COMPOSITION.

(1) Expand the outline No. 2 on p. 115 of your English book.

(2) Write out the first portion of the story given in Exercise 10, on p. 129, continue it, and add your own conclusion.

Select any two of the following subjects, prepare them, and then write out fully in your exercise books.

(1) Your speech as Captain of the School Football Team on being presented with the League Cup.

(2) A letter to a chum congratulating him on winning a scholarship.

(3) Indications of the approach of spring.

(4) A letter to a boy in India, describing a hard winter in England.

GRAMMAR.

(1) Punctuate passages 6 and 7 in Exercise 1, p. 59.

(2) Change parts 1 and 2 of Exercise 2, p. 61, from direct into reported speech.

SPECIAL LESSON.

On Wednesday; March 1st, at 9.30 a.m., a lesson will be given on "Direct and Reported Speech." All Standard VII boys must be present.

MATHEMATICS AND SCIENCE

March

STUDY.

(1) Learn the note on Ratio at the top of p. 12, Cambridge Arithmetic; that on Profit and Loss on p. 16; and that on Simple Interest on p. 18.

(2) Write out and learn the two formulae for the triangle given on p. 26, and the formulae for the cylinder and cone on pp. 30 and 31.

(3) Read the notes on p. 37 on commission and brokerage, and those on pp. 64 and 65 on the areas of irregular figures.

WRITTEN WORK.

Work examples:
(1) 3, 15, 18, 21, p. 10 Camb. Arith.
(2) 1, 2, 3, 4, 5, 21, 22, 23, p. 11, Camb. Arith.
(3) 1, 2, 3, p. 12, Camb. Arith.
(4) 1, 2, 3, p. 13, Camb. Arith.
(5) 4, 5, 6, p. 14, Camb. Arith.
(6) 1, 2, 5, p. 17, Camb. Arith.
(7) 1, 3, 6, p. 18, Camb. Arith.
(8) Work example 3 (Fig. 4) on p. 65, and calculate the area of the deck of the vessel.

EXPERIMENTAL SCIENCE

Work out and describe two or more of the experiments from Lessons 6 and 7 on the cone and cylinder.

Study Lesson 13 on Specific Gravity, and copy the drawing on p. 12. McDougall's Handwork Science, Book II.

Now let me point out some of the advantages of this individual method of teaching.

1. The child's individuality is recognized, studied, and cultivated.

2. Every child can go at his own pace. No child is hindered by having to wait for others; the slow child is not hurried beyond his powers, and so does better and more lasting work.

3. The child with a tendency to be lazy becomes interested by being allowed more choice.

4. Work is done *by* the child, instead of *for* him; he gains experience by doing, and has the satisfaction of accomplishing something by his own efforts.

5. There is no breaking off a piece of work just when it is most interesting, nor continuing it when bored or fatigued.

6. There is unity in the teaching. If a child is absent for a week or two he takes up the work on his return just where he left off; he does not lose the thread of his subject, as so often happens in class teaching.

7. The children in each room form a family group; the older and more advanced children help the younger and weaker ones whenever they are appealed to, without telling them too much, or making them too dependent. This cultivates a helping spirit in the older pupils, and at the same time fixes their own knowledge more firmly in their minds, as all teaching does.

8. There is no sharp break with the method of study in after-school life.

9. There is no marking time when a child reaches Standard VII, no matter how few children there are in that standard.

10. Children being free to work at a subject when they feel most inclined are keener, more alert, and attack and overcome difficulties much more readily.

11. A child's organizing powers are developed by having to plan out and complete his monthly programme in the given time.

12. Friendly emulation is aroused; the younger children work hard to catch up to the older ones, and the older ones are anxious to keep ahead.

13. There is closer personal contact between teacher and pupil.

14. There is no difficulty with promotion; every child is promoted as soon as he is ready.

15. For the last year or so of a child's school life he may be allowed to do a minimum of work in those subjects for which he has little or no aptitude, and then his education and training can

be carried on mainly through those subjects in which he is keenly interested.

This copy of the time-table will give a good idea as to the subjects taken in classes in the afternoons.

Four equal divisions, containing in all from 160 to 200 children, are arranged on an age basis:

Division 1 ages 13 and 14.
Division 2 ages 12 and 13.
Division 3 ages 11 and 12.
Division 4 ages 9, 10, 11.

SUBJECTS.

As indicated, rambles for Nature study or sketching, or lantern lectures on geography or history, are specially arranged, and the times entered in the log book under "Science." A course of hygiene and temperance is taken, and experimental work in physical science is demonstrated. As the divisions do not correspond to the standards, the teacher takes experimental and oral work in science and mathematics with small groups, while the others work as in a morning.

Elocution and dramatization are taken in the literature and oral reading lessons. The literature is taught in classes, so is scripture. It is in these lessons where the personality of the teacher in his translation of the author's words and thoughts and spirit has the greatest effect on the imagination and emotions of the children. The literature is taken on the lines given in my book, *Literature Teaching in Schools*—A Manual of Matter and Method (published by E. J. Arnold, Leeds, at 4*s*. 6*d*. net). It covers eight years of a child's school life.

A weekly debate is taken in Division 1, the subject and leaders being decided upon by the children a week beforehand. This practises the older ones in thinking while on their feet, and trains them in giving suitable and logical expression to their thoughts—an exercise which experience of listening to speakers in other spheres of life shows to be very necessary.

Handwriting includes writing, figuring, and general style. This corrects any tendency to slovenly work, which may occur when children are more intent upon the subject matter under consideration than they are on the neatness of the form in which they express it; though if very careless work is brought to be examined under the Dalton Plan in a morning, the teacher puts his pen through it, and then the exercise has to be re-written. This leads the child to see not only that what is worth doing at all is worth doing well, but that slovenly, dirty, or untidy work of any kind is an act of discourtesy to the person to whom it is presented.

Physical training and music are taken by a specialist teacher, and are taught in the age divisions—a much better classification for these subjects than that of the standards.

THE TIME-TABLE.

MORNING.

9 TO 9.30.	9.30 TO 12.
Religious Instruction.	*Dalton Plan of Individual Teaching.* *Vertical Classification of Children in Standards IV to VIII.* Academic Subjects are taken in the appointed rooms under Specialist Teachers.

In the Hall ... ... Reading.
In Room 1 ... ... Art.
In Room 2 ... ... Geography and History.
In Room 3 ... ... English.
In Room 4 ... ... Mathematics.
In Room 5 ... ... Science and Handicraft.

Recreation—10.45 to 11.

Special Handicraft Instruction: Wednesday, a.m., Standard VI; Thursday, a.m., Standard V; Friday, a.m., Standards VII and VIII.

AFTERNOON.

Div.	1.30 TO 2.15.	2.15 TO 2.45.	DAY.	3 TO 3.30.	3.30 TO 4.
1	Music	Handwriting	Mon.	Science and Maths.	Oral Reading
2	Handwriting	Music		Oral Reading	Science and Maths.
3	Literature	Science and Maths.		} Music	
4	Science and Maths.	Literature			(Songs)

AFTERNOON—*continued.*

Div.	1.30 to 2.15.	2.15 to 2.45.	Day.	3 to 3.30.	3.30 to 4.
1 2 3 4	Physical Training Literature Science and Maths. Oral Reading	Literature Physical Training Oral Reading Science and Maths.	Tues.	Science and Maths. Handwriting Physical Training Literature	Debate Science and Maths. Literature Physical Training
	Academic Subjects taken as in Mornings		Wed.	SPORTS. Academic Subjects are taken in bad weather	
1 2 3 4	Literature Science and Maths. Music Handwriting	Science and Maths. Literature Handwriting Music	Thur.	} Music Science and Maths. Oral Reading	(Songs) Oral Reading Science and Maths.
1 2 3 4	Physical Training Literature Science and Maths. Handwriting	Literature Physical Training Handwriting Science and Maths.	Fri.	Science and Maths. Oral Reading Physical Training Literature	Oral Reading Science and Maths. Literature Physical Training

RECREATION—2.45 to 3.

Classification is according to age.
Elocution and dramatization are taken by the teachers of Literature and Reading.
Rambles and Lantern Lectures are taken by special arrangement.

Now I will give a number of questions put and criticisms offered by visitors, and append my answers to them.

1. Is not the constant application a strain upon the children?

   We have not found it so. Children can change their subject when they are tired of it. After close study or written work a child can go into the art room, or into the reading room, where he can read an interesting story or a collection of stories, or into the science and handicraft room, and do some experimenting, or make a model in plasticine or cardboard of something about which he has been reading. This relieves any possibility of a strain.

2. But what about the nerve strain upon the teacher?

   Certainly, the teacher is kept hard at work throughout the morning session, but he has the management of his subject in his own hands. He can vary his corrections of written work with questions on the subject matter set for study; he can take a few children round the blackboard for sectional instruction on some weak point, or he can go among the boys and chat with them about their work. These variations will be found quite effective.

3. How do you prevent boys wasting their time while waiting to be marked?

   Each boy who has his work ready to be marked writes his name on the blackboard and then goes on with further work. The teacher calls out one boy at a time in the order of names on the blackboard.

4. Do you find children wandering aimlessly about from one room to another?

No. Most boys stay in a room for an hour or more. We encourage them to finish a written answer, map, drawing, or composition, when they have begun it, before going on with any other subject.

5. Are your text-books all suitable?

They are the best we can get for the time being. When there is a greater demand for text-books suitable for young children publishers will respond to it. Teachers should examine the newest catalogues and choose for themselves.

6. Do you find any children slacking under the new arrangement?

They cannot slack without being found out. Their Work Record Card shows what they have done in each subject, and they can be asked to produce it at any time by any teacher. Then again, by a glance at his own Record Book a teacher can see at once if any boy is neglecting his subject, and can call him up for interview. But the tendency is all the other way. The difficulty is to get children to give up work at recreation time and home time. Many of them work at home of their own free will, as no home lessons are given.

7. How do you manage when too many children wish to go into a certain room at the same time?

Preference is given to those who are less advanced in the subject, and to those who have only that subject to finish in order to complete the month's work. The teacher tells the children that he wants six, eight, or ten, as the case may be, to volunteer to go to another room for the present; and a sufficient number goes immediately without demur. It is good training in self-denial.

8. Will not oral work suffer under this plan?
There is ample opportunity for oral work and for speech training in the afternoon class lessons, as will be seen from the time-table; and in the morning session conversation is frequent among the children themselves, and between teacher and child.

9. What happens when a child loses his Work Record Card?
He has to pay a penny for a new one, and also has to take the trouble to get the teachers to initial his work over again. This means that he loses time and money as well as his card, and so he is very careful with it. Few have been lost.

10. Do you find that the style of the written work deteriorates?
Very little. There is a special lesson in the afternoon given to correct any tendency in this direction. Moreover, slovenly work done in the morning session has to be re-written, and so the children learn by experience that what is worth doing at all is worth doing well.

11. Do you intend bringing any of the lower standards into this scheme?

Possibly Standard III; but, according to our present judgment, not below that, though the methods in Standards I and II will, in some subjects, particularly the three R's, be largely individual. It must be remembered that the Dalton Plan is not the Montessori System.

12. Has the freedom allowed had any adverse effect on discipline?

On the contrary, it is a great aid to discipline; it is a training in responsibility and self-control. When children are interested and have plenty to do there is no trouble with discipline.

13. Have you lockers for the boys?

No. All have school bags, and each one carries his own books and writing materials; each teacher concerned keeps a check on them. Material for art work, handicraft and experimental science are stored in cupboards in the allotted rooms. Boys get them as they want them and return them to the proper places when they have done with them.

14. How do you deal with a child who has been absent, say, for three months?

We let him continue at the place where he left off, but we lessen the amount of work in most subjects so as to give him an opportunity to recover the lost ground as soon as possible.

15. How do you deal with a child who is very backward, say, in arithmetic, and fairly well up in the other subjects?

He is allotted easier work in that subject. If necessary, he is given work in it that is a standard lower. In fact, the work is made to fit him. We do not attempt the impossible task of making him fit the work.

16. How does a boy proceed when he has completed all his subjects for the month with one exception, and on going to the particular room where that subject is taken he finds all the places occupied?

Such a boy is allowed to go to the teacher of that subject, and tell him his work for the next month is being held up because he has not completed that subject. The teacher asks someone whose work is not so urgent to give way, and that is invariably done.

17. You allow boys to talk and move about during work time. Do you find any truth in the old saying: "Give them an inch and they will take a yard?"

The saying is true enough in the case of children who have been subjected to the old military discipline. Like children whose parents have ruled them with a rod of iron, and like army men, when the restrictions are removed reaction sets in, and its violence is usually proportionate to the preceding pressure. It is not true in the case of children brought up under saner methods. Certainly we allow children to talk and move about. They must do that if they are to help one another. But the rule is that all conversation must be in whispers, and movement from one part of a room to another must be for a definite purpose connected with the subject. We do not find the privilege abused.

18. Is not the Dalton Plan swinging the pendulum too far in the opposite direction from that in which the teacher did nearly all the work?

Not with our arrangement and method. The teacher does a good deal in the way of advice, help, guidance, and encouragement, only it is done with the individual instead of with the mass—a much more impressive and effective method. And this is in addition to the sectional and class lessons which are given on new work, or in special points in the subjects set for study.

19. When do you allow more freedom of choice as regards subjects?

At present, when a boy has finished his work for Standard VII, allotments of mathematics and English only are given to him, sufficient to occupy six or seven days during the month. The remaining time is spent on favourite subjects; the only requirement is that a record of work done shall be kept, and that such work shall be examined by the teachers of those subjects. In special cases this plan may be adopted for children who have not completed, and never will complete, the work of Standard VII.

20. My fears are that the inspiration and enthusiasm which passes from teacher to pupils in class teaching will disappear under the Dalton Plan. What is your view?

It is true that in some lessons, and particularly with some teachers, subtle influences pass from teacher to children when they are taught in the mass; but scripture, literature, music, and some history lessons are almost the only subjects where that happens, and under our scheme these are taken in class lessons. I am of opinion that the influence of a teacher's conversation with an individual child on any ordinary academic subject is much more potent than what is said in a class lesson. Those of us who are older often hear sermons or lectures which inspire us, and if we are privileged to talk over points with the preacher or lecturer afterwards, the effect is much more emphatic and permanent. But how many class lessons have children to listen to which are boring and useless, and others where they are not sufficiently interested to ask a question? If we use class teaching and individual work in their proper places the best results will follow.

APPENDICES

APPENDIX I

ASSIGNMENTS WHICH HAVE BEEN USED IN BRITISH ELEMENTARY SCHOOLS

FOUR ASSIGNMENTS

FROM 'AN ELEMENTARY SCHOOL FOR BOYS WHERE THE TEACHERS SPECIALIZE

HISTORY. CONTRACT 3.

First Assignment   *Standard VII*

1st Period

The British Empire is one "on which the sun never sets." It comprises vast self-governing colonies, like Canada, Australia, New Zealand, and South Africa; great dependencies like India, large protectorates like Egypt, and wide-spreading possessions like Uganda and Nigeria. How was this great Empire built up? To answer this question fully and well will be our history for the present year. I am sure you will be more than interested to read stories of daring adventure showing the dogged spirit of discoverers and colonists to bear want, and overcome difficulty; a strong sense of right and justice on the part of the British race, all of which, coupled with deeds of valour, glorious victories on land and sea, and brilliant statesmanship at home, have combined to make this Empire what it is to-day. The little Mother-country of England contains only 50,222 square miles, and yet the British Empire to-day consists of nearly 14,000,000 square miles of territory. The existence of Greater Britain as a State depends upon her maintaining the control of the seas, and it therefore follows that our history must begin at that period when there was great rivalry between England and other nations for the discovery of sea-routes to new lands.

This week I am asking you to read:

"The Story of Christopher Columbus," "Piers Plowman," Book 3, pp. 54–61, "Christopher Columbus, and the first Voyage to America," "Three famous Voyages," pp. 5–8.

This will count for two days' work. Answer the questions below, and these will count for three days' work.

Questions:

1. Make a sketch map showing the known world before the voyage of Columbus.
2. Give an account of the early life of Columbus.
3. Who discovered the Cape of Good Hope?
4. How did it get its name?

Show all your work to me before you mark it upon your cards, and do this with all the written work.

2nd Period

We shall continue this week the story of Christopher Columbus and the first voyage to America. "Three famous Voyages," pp. 8–24.

The reading will count for two days' work, and the questions are three days' work.

Questions:

1. Draw a map to show the course Columbus took on his voyage to America.
2. Write a short story of the voyage of Columbus to America.

3rd Period

The Tudor period is called "the Age of Discovery," and all the sovereigns of this period showed their interest in the new lands. It was the beginning of our great Empire.

Read: "Trade and Discovery," "Columbus and Cabot," "Self Help History," pp. 38-44.

This is a day's work; the questions given below will count for four days' work.

Questions:

1. Why is the Tudor period called the Age of Discovery?
2. Name the two countries most anxious to discover a sea-route to India.
3. Say how they set about the task.
4. Why were the new sea-routes necessary?
5. What do you know of the Cabots and their famous voyages?

4th Period

We are going to read the story of how the Portuguese were the first to double the Cape of Good Hope and discovered a sea-route to India.

The reading will be three days' work, and the questions will make up the other two days.

Read: "Vasco da Gama and the first voyage to India round the Cape of Good Hope," "Three famous Voyages," pp. 25-47.

Questions:

1. Draw a map illustrating Vasco da Gama's voyage to India.
2. Give the names of the three vessels and their commanders.
3. Who was Davane? Why were his services valuable to Da Gama?

ENGLISH LITERATURE. CONTRACT 1.
First Assignment *Standard V*

1st Period

This month's job will be to make a study of the Ballad.

A Ballad is a simple spirited poem which tells graphically some well-known incident.

Repeat to yourself the nursery rhyme:

> "Old King Cole was a merry old soul,
> And a merry old soul was he."

Count the number of syllables in each line, and the number of accents. When you read the three Ballads we have chosen you will find they were written in this old metre—it is the popular ballad metre.

"The Revenge" (A Ballad of the Fleet), Tennyson (Boys' Book of Poetry, III).

1. Before you read the poem take from the shelf in the history room "Scenes from Tudor Times." You will find on page 130 a most interesting account of the last fight of the *Revenge* by Sir Walter Raleigh, who was alive when the events took place and had first-hand information. Tennyson based his poem on this account. Read Raleigh's story carefully. When you read the poem you will be

pleased to find how cleverly the poet has turned the story into verse. (This is one day's work.)

Note: Whenever you read a poem:

1. Read it straight through. Get a general idea of the thoughts it contains, and enter into the rhythm or beat of the verse. Do not stop over words you do not understand.
2. Now go over the poem again. Do not pass over any word or passage you do not understand. Your dictionary will help a good deal. Above all, *think* about the difficulty, try to get at the idea which lies behind the words. Write down a list of the words you have had to look up and learn them.
3. Now read the poem straight through again. You will enjoy it more on account of the clearer understanding with which you will be able to read it.
4. Read the poem in the way suggested. Find the Azores on your map (off the coast of America). If you find any difficulty you cannot solve ask about it. (This is two days' work.)
5. Imagine you were one of the crew of the *Revenge.* Write an account of the fight. (This is two days' work.)

Hand in your book when you have completed the composition.

2nd Period

"The Defence of Lucknow," Tennyson (Boys' Book of Poetry, III).

1. Take from the history room Warner's "Survey of British History." Read the account of the Indian Mutiny, pp. 222–225. You will then understand how the men, women, and children became shut up in Lucknow. Notice who the leader of the defence was, and who led the relieving force. (One day's work.)

2. Read the poem in the way suggested last week. (Two days' work.)
3. Write down any lines which you think specially striking. If you can, add a note saying why you think them fine. (One day's work.)
4. Can you see any ways in which the poet makes the story vivid? If so, say what they are, and illustrate with lines from the poem. (One day's work.)

Hand in your book when you have completed this poem.

3rd Period

"The Last of the Eurydice," J. N. Paton (Boys' Book of Poetry, II).

1. Read the poem in the way suggested. Note the metre.
2. Follow on a map the homeward course of the ship from the Indian Sea. Find all places mentioned on the map.
3. Notice how the poem falls naturally into the following sections:

     Verses 1–2. Introduction.
     Verses 3–5. The journey home.
     Verses 6–8. The coming of the storm.
     Verse   9. The wreck.

A poem which tells a story always follows some such definite plan.

4. Write an account of the breaking of the storm. (Imagine you are Fletcher.) (This will count as five days' work.)

4th Period

Commit to memory "The Last of the Eurydice." Report to me when you know it. (Four days' work.)

Note what was said about the sections into which a "story poem" can be divided. Treat "The Revenge" in the same way as I did the "Eurydice."

Write the divisions in your book. (One day's work.) Hand in your book when you have finished.

ARITHMETIC. CONTRACT 1.

First Assignment   *Standard V*

1st Period

This month you will spend chiefly in revision of Standard IV work. Revision simply means doing some work that you have already done once, over again, to make sure you have not forgotten it.

Let us see what you already know. You know something about Fractions and Simple Decimals. You also know the Long Rules. By Long Rules we mean long multiplication and long divisions, that is, multiplication and division by bigger numbers than 12 without using factors.

For the first week's work, then, you will revise the Long Rules. In MacDougall's "Suggestive Arithmetic," Book 5, you will find examples of multiplication and division worked for you on page 2. Study these carefully, and ask me about anything you don't understand. Then work at least three sums out of each of the exercises A and B. That will count for two days' work. Then work Exercise 5 in the "New Sovereign Arithmetic," Book 5, either X or Y. That will be three days' work.

As soon as you have finished an exercise bring it out to be corrected.

2nd Period

The second week's work will still be revision of Long Rules, but this time you will multiply and divide sums of money, weights, and measures, etc.

In MacDougall's "Suggestive Arithmetic," Book 5 (in future we will call them just "suggestive") you will find several examples worked for you on pages 4 and 6. Read these carefully and then work one sum

of each kind out of the exercises. You should then
be able to turn to page 11 and work either A, B, or
C. If you prefer it, work either X or Y of Exercise
25 in the "New Sovereign," page 7.

3rd Period

There are some short ways of multiplying and dividing by certain numbers. You will find some of them
mentioned on page 11 of "Elementary Workshop
Arithmetic." Pay particular attention to multiplying
and dividing by 25 and 125. In some of these you will
have to use your knowledge of Decimals.

For the first two days, make up some easy examples
of your own in the short multiplication and division by
25 and 125. You can test your answers by the long
method. For the next three days' work read what it
says about Measures of Numbers in "New Sovereign,"
5, and work X or Y of Exercise 27.

4th Period

For this fourth week's work you will learn what it
says on page 9 of "New Sovereign," 5, about Multiples
of Numbers.

There are two ways of finding the L.C.M. I think
the second way (by factors) is the easier for what you
want. You will find this work useful when you come
to do Addition and Subtraction of Vulgar Fractions.

Learning the meaning of the terms, and understanding the examples given, counts for two days' work.

Exercise 28 (either X or Y) is one day's work.

Exercise 29 (either X or Y) is two days' work.

NATURE, SCIENCE, AND DRAWING. CONTRACT 2.
First Assignment   *Standard VI*

1st Period

1. The first subject for study is the working of soil.
   You have seen men digging, hoeing, raking, and

weeding gardens and allotments, but do you know why they do it? You will be able to gather some useful information from "The Vegetable Garden," chap. v. This is one day's work. When you have read the chapter write down the reasons for trenching heavy soil. (This is two days' work.)

2. Construct a scale 1 in. to 1 ft. and draw the front of the cupboard to that scale. (This is two days' work.)

3. Draw the objects set up for you. (One day's work.)

2nd Period

1. Last week you learned the value of working soil, and how it enabled plants to get at their food. This week we shall find out what that food consists of. Read the paragraph on the Plant Foods, page 36 in the "Vegetable Garden," as far as "cheapness of them" on page 43.

  Answer questions 14 and 15 on page 49. (This will count for two days' work.)

2. Construct a scale 1½ in. to 1 ft. and draw the blackboard to scale. (This is two days' work.)

3. Draw the objects set up. (This is one day's work.)

3rd Period

1. This week we continue the study of Plant Foods. You must gather what you can from page 43 about Fertilizers. Read to the end of the chapter. (This is one day's work.) Answer question 10 on page 49. (This will count for another day's work.)

2. Construct a scale 2 in. to 1 ft. to read 4 foot and showing inches. Draw to that scale the top of your desk. (This is two days' work.)

3. Select an object at home, study it carefully and draw it from memory at school.

4th Period

1. This week I want you to learn all you can about farmyard manure. You must read pages 40–43. (One day's work.) Answer me the following questions in your books:

   What are the chief plant foods and what effect each has on plants? (This is one day's work.)
2. Take a scale of 1 in. to 1 yard and draw a plan of the room. (This is two days' work.)
3. Draw the objects set up for you.

ASSIGNMENTS

FROM SEVERAL ELEMENTARY SCHOOLS WHERE THE TEACHERS SPECIALIZE

Contract II 1922   HISTORY   *Class II*

1st Week

Our last contract closed with a study of Town Life in early Tudor days; we shall now note the changes that are seen by the end of the period. Study "Town Life in Queen Elizabeth's Days," chap. vii. p. v. In your note-book set out a clear statement of the changes, and account for them. Come to me for extra reading.

2nd Week

We shall now begin a study of the changes in religion and how they affected the people. Study chap. iii, p. v, "The Dissolution of the Monasteries." Learn the answers to these questions:

What good work had monasteries done during the warlike Middle Ages?

Why were they no longer so greatly needed?

Why did Henry VIII want to get rid of them?

How did he set about it? What happened to priors, monks, building land, other treasures, *e.g.*, books, plate, carved oak?

What did the poor think about it?

3rd Week

Let us now consider the changes in the parish churches from chap. iv, p. v. Find out and jot down the condition of the Church and its services before the Reformation?

After the Reformation?

Notice that now the King was Head of the Church, fresh changes came with every new sovereign. Place a record of the changes under the name of each sovereign in whose reign they took place.

4th Week

This week I want you to read all you can about Wolsey. Begin with "Builders of History," Book III. He is an example of a great churchman in the days before the Reformation, when churchmen took also high positions in the State. Other books about Wolsey shall be placed on the table.

GEOGRAPHY

Last month's contract gave us a study of Highlands. This month we will consider the Lowland countries of Holland and Belgium. Read in Palmer's "Europe," p. 92, the chapter on an ocean conquest, to see what a fight the Dutch had to win and secure their land from the sea. Study from the next chapter the appearance of this flat land and the work of the Dutch upon it. Learn points of interest about the towns from pp. 88, 89, and all there is about Holland in T.B.

2nd Week

This week I want you to read as many descriptive extracts about Holland as you can, then depict in words:

"A Dutch Scene" as Composition in Geography.

Note-books. The books available will be indicated on board.

3rd Week

I should like every girl to read chap. vii in the little green book "Europe and Britain"; and also to study Belgium from Palmer, pp. 103, 108, and from Townley, as well as from T.B.

Jot down the reasons for her being such a prosperous little country. Read all you can about Brussels, Bruges, Ghent, Antwerp, Namur, Liège, Mons.

4th Week

This week we will take some practical map work. Trace the outlines of Scandinavia, the Netherlands, France, and Switzerland, separately; paste the tracings on cardboard and cut out. All maps of countries should be on the same scale so that you can fit them together. This will help you to visualize their shape and their relation to one another. Still continue to read stories and extracts about the western countries of Europe.

Group 4   GEOGRAPHY   *Standard IV*

1st Month

I. Position of England in world. (Old lesson.)
   Study chap. i, Lay's "British Isles."
Questions:
   1. Why is it cooler in England than in Africa?
   2. Why are there fishing towns on the east coast of British Isles?

3. Why has Britain become the greatest naval power in the world?

II. ORAL LESSON. Making of weather chart.
Question: Trace outline map of England; shade places where wheat is grown.
III. Study chap. ii, pp. 12–15, in "Human Geography."
      ORAL LESSON. Orchard lands.
   1. On outline map shade in parts where fruit is grown.
   2. Show what the fruit farmers' work is from spring to autumn.
   3. Explain why fruit is grown so plentifully in Kent.

2nd Month

1. ORAL LESSON. Making of weather chart. (For those who have completed previous syllabus.)
Questions:
   1. Draw a map of south-east England and put in the high ground and the orchard lands.
   2. Copy the diagrams showing the positions of Canterbury and Maidstone.
II. Study chap. iii, pp. 22, 26, "Pennine Moorlands."
   1. Describe a journey from the valleys up to the Pennine moorlands.
III. Study chap. iii, pp. 26–29, "Pennine Moorlands."
   1. Draw a map of the Pennine moorlands, showing and naming gaps, and mark in the railways.
IV. Test.

3rd Month

ORAL LESSON LIST.
   1. The course of a river: its uses.
   2. Contour lines: how they are made from model.
   3. Interpretation of contour lines or how to understand what a country looks like by looking at contour lines (mountains, valleys, etc.).

PRIVATE STUDY.

I. Study chap. iv, pp. 30–33.

Make notes on following questions:

1. Why must a market town be in a good position for trade? Say what you think a good position means.
2. Explain the position of York. Show why the Romans and Normans chose it as a town and built a castle there. Name the river flowing through it.
3. What kind of things would you expect to find on sale at York?
4. Draw diagram showing position of York.

II. Study pp. 33–38. Answer some questions on Carlisle and Lancaster as were asked about York.

Note why counties were divided into shires and what marked the divisions.

III. Study pp. 41–44. Make notes on woollen manufacture: (a) at home, (b) in factories. Use Encyclopedia, pp. 26, 262, 359, 750.

4th Month

I. Drawing of sections from contour map.

Study pp. 43–46 and make notes on the manufacture of cotton goods from the growing of cotton to the finishing of the cloth.

II. Short oral lesson on "Docks." Study pp. 47–51.

(a) Why is it necessary to have harbours—what kind of things do ships carry to and from England?
Why is water transport cheaper than land?
Describe or draw two kinds of harbours.
What part of a river is called the estuary?
What is a "Dry Dock"; what kind of work is done there?

III. Study pp. 51–58.
 1. Why is the Humber estuary very suitable for a port?
    What is the port there and what trade does it do?
 2. Why is the estuary of the Mersey a good place for a cotton port?
    On what part of the river is Liverpool?
 3. Why was Liverpool unimportant until recently, and why has it now become second in importance?
 4. What is meant by exports and imports?
 5. Which is the biggest cotton market? Why was the Manchester Ship Canal cut?

IV.
 1. Why is Newcastle an important town?
    (a) Note position at important cross roads.
    (b) Note estuary.
    (c) Note work done.
 2. Where does food for factory towns come from?
 3. Make notes on fishing—say where each kind is found: (a) those caught with a drift net, (b) those caught with hook.
 4. What are fishing smacks and trawlers?
 5. Copy fig. 19, p. 58, showing Dogger Bank, Yarmouth Roads, and fishing towns.

ENGLISH (10 years)

3rd Week

COMPOSITION.

A Description. If it is well done I shall be able to picture it in my mind, seeing every little detail—just as you were able to do in the sentences of last week's language lesson.

Now, of course, it is impossible to give me something you don't possess. So it is ABSOLUTELY NECESSARY that you should have a clear picture before you write a word.

Choose your subject, then forget everything else, close your eyes, and let the picture form into shape. Do not stop at the first flash, but stay till you have every detail, just as though you were on the spot really looking.

Choose your subject from the following:

1. Describe the scene at a busy railway station.
2. Describe a house on fire.
3. (For A and B only.) Describe any particular place on an autumn morning.

LANGUAGE.

The lesson this week needs careful thought.

1st Day. Study the sentences given on pp. 39–40 (Lesson 18).

Think over the words given in black type. They show you something very useful to you in your composition. By changing a word a little, we may give it another use. In the words given you, notice the change made. With these words notice how we can compare things.

You are to stop at the line on p. 41, and do the exercise on p. 41.

2nd Day. Study the rest of the lesson. There is something very important to learn here. Find out what it is and learn before Thursday, when I shall ask you about it. Do Exercise VII.

READING.

Chaps. 6, 7, 8.

Read through the questions, to remind yourself first. Make a list of all the words you do not know the meaning of. Try to find out by the way it is used in the book or by asking.

ENGLISH

Class IV. (Average age 10 years)

4th Week

COMPOSITION.

A Description.

Turn to p. 50, N.E. Books. Read through the whole of Lesson 22, picturing each little description.

Now think about your subject for the week. Close your eyes and picture it. Arrange your time so that you do this just before you have an opportunity of actually studying it. Compare your mind picture with the real one. See where your thoughts were clear, and study the hazy ideas carefully to get those clear too. Every little detail must appear in your description.

Do not forget that you cannot describe well without good, fitting adjectives. Lesson 9 will give you illustrations of this:

SUBJECTS:

(a) Describe someone whom you know well.
(b) Describe the picture of the Red Indian Chiefs round their camp fire.

LANGUAGE.

Joining words. Lesson 19.

After this lesson you will be privileged to use "and" and "but" in joining sentences. In most cases you have used these words, especially "and," badly and repeatedly.

Study the sentences on p. 43. Find out when "and" is the best word for joining. *Find out why.* You will now be able to make use of it in a similar way in your compositions. Study the use of "but" as a joining word. It is only the best word for joining when used in this way.

You may complete the sentences on the next page using "and" or "but" correctly. Write them in your private notebooks.

Third day's language will be a test on the work you have studied during the month.

READING.

Complete "The Cuckoo Clock."
Answer the questions (on paper).

Div. I (*a*)   ENGLISH   *Contract I*

ASSIGNMENT 2 (age 13)

This week we shall continue with Sentence Structure (see Lesson 5).

The model paragraph given illustrates the use of two classes of verbs. What are they? What is their effect?

Notice further that action denoted by a Transitive Verb can be expressed in two ways. These two forms of the Transitive Verb secure variety in structure.

Examine the paragraph carefully, and analyse its build. Then write the answer to Exercise I, p. 42.

The Essay which you prepared in the rough last week must come in this week in its finished state.

ADDITIONAL WORK FOR KEEN PEOPLE.

Change the following sentences from loose to periodic, and state the difference in emphasis:

1. The child pocketed the money and tucked the bread under his thin little arm, and trudged out of the shop.
2. Just then she covered her face with her hands, for she could not bear to watch the ascent.

3. He waited, standing in a bright spot, surrounded by glittering windows filled with bright colours.

4. It had been snowing in a leisurely way all the long dreary day, so that the roofs and window-sills of the tiny scattered cottages in the little village on the mountain were piled high with thick white covers of spotless snow.

ASSIGNMENT 3

You should enjoy the study set for this week, its title suggests pleasure. Extract all the beauty that lurks in the example before you in Lesson 6, and *feel* the power of the figures of speech illustrated.

R. L. Stevenson was a master of the art of hitting upon the most striking comparison. In your reading, especially of his works, be always on the look-out for illustrations.

Answer Exercise I, p. 46, writing one thought about each idea. State in each case whether you have used Metaphor or Simile.

ESSAY. Stevenson says we get entertainment pretty much in proportion as we give. And this is one reason why the world is dull to dull persons. Illustrate this thought. See "An Inland Voyage."

Class II   4 ASSIGNMENTS   *Contract II*

(Girls aged 11 and 12 years)

ARITHMETIC ASSIGNMENT

I.
1. What do you understand by the Metric System?
2. Write the prefixes which denote 100 times, $\frac{1}{1000}$, $\frac{1}{10}$, 10 times, and $\frac{1}{100}$.
3. What is the Metric unit of (1) capacity, (2) weight, (3) coinage, (4) length?

4. What is the English equivalent of (1) a litre, (2)
   a kilogramme, (3) a metre?

Work Loney, page 70. Nos. 1, 2, 3, 4, 5.
  "   "   "   "   "   9, 10, 11, 12.
  "   "   "   "   "   13, 14, 15, 16.

II.

What is a multiple of a given number?

What do you understand by "a common multiple of
   two or more numbers"?

What is the least Common Multiple of such numbers?

What is a prime number?

How do you find the L.C.M. of two prime numbers?

Give the L.C.M. of 4 and 5, 8 and 9, 1 and 7, 14 and
   15, 19 and 3, 16 and 7, 24 and 13.

Break up the following numbers into their prime
   factors: 18, 104, 35, 26, 32, 96, 54.

What is the L.C.M. of 4 and 6, 9 and 6, 2 and 9, 8
   and 12, 21 and 9, 35 and 15, 21 and 49, 24 and
   35?

Work Loney, page 22. Nos. 1, 2, 3, 4.
  "   "   "   "   "   5, 6, 7, 8, 9, 10.

III.

What do you understand by (1) a proper fraction,
   (2) an improper fraction, (3) a mixed number?

Work Loney, page 27. Nos. 4–9.
  "   "   "   27.   "   15–20.
  "   "   "   29.   "   1–8.
  "   "   "   30.   "   4–8.
  "   "   "   30.   "   9–12, 14.

IV.

Work Loney, page 31. Nos. 12–16.
  "   "   "   31.   "   21–25.
  "   "   "   32.   "   15–22.
  "   "   "   33.   "   19–23.
  "   "   "   33.   "   41–44.

CONTRACT ASS

	ARITHMETIC.	HISTORY.		
	GENERAL TESTS, TO INCLUDE AT LEAST FIVE SUMS.	PREP.	TESTS.	HAN
Jan. 13	*Memorize.* Easy Decimals and Percentages. *Revise.* { Clock Sums. Race Sums. Speed Sums. *Tots.* Practice, 3. *Study.* Proportional Tests. *General Tests.* 3.	Write complete notes on France throughout the century: Settlement, 1815; Revol. agst. Absolutism; Revol. agst. Capitalism; Revol. agst. Imperialism; A Republic.	Write an account of the French Revolutionary Wars under Periods.	Mak of Batt Traf Wat
20	*Practical.* Model to show: { Long, Square, Cub. Meas. *Revise.* { S. and C. Interest. S. and C. Proportion. *Study.* Metric System. *Speed Test.* Std. IV, ½ hr. *General Tests.* 2.	Draw up a chart of the Revolutions in Europe in 1830, 1848. Give Causes and Results.	Compare the methods of govt. in European Countries in 1815–1919. Explain and give dates of changes.	Draw ou su illus of E Hi 1815
27	*Memorize.* Wide Measure. *Revise.* { Reductions. Bringing to dec. and %, Irreg. Areas. *Study.* Exchange Sums. *Speed Test.* Mechan. Rates. *General Tests.* 2.	Write notes on the Coloni- zation of Europ. Countries in Asia, Africa, America.	Explain in *own words* six important European Treaties. Dates, Clauses.	On a the show colo Eu Cou
Feb. 3	*Practical.* Draw to scale: H. water, { Allow Ceiling, { fireplace, Floor. { window. *Revise.* { L.C.M., H.C.F., Practice, Red. of V.F.'s, D.F. of %. *Study.* Stocks. *Speed Test.* Std. V. *General Tests.* 2.	Make a chart, showing chief events of century, in Germany, Italy, England, France, Russia.	Show why the period after 1870 is called the Era of Alliances.	Mak mo a Bat Aer Sub

SUPPLEMENTARY

One hour extra per week may b

Individual records must be kept

, JANUARY, 1922.

OGRAPHY.		ENGLISH.	LITERATURE.
TESTS.	HANDWORK.		
Name a region of: Enterprise, Backwardness, Large Popul., Waste, Advantages, Disadvantages. Describe them.	Draw a Route Map of World, showing Cargoes.	*Debate.* Girl Guides. *Essay.* Washington Conference. *Reply to following·* Office boy, smart, good handwriting, accurate figures. Apply, stating full particulars, to C. Kent and Co., 4 High St., Boston. *Write* a few lines to illustrate all punctuation marks you know.	"Fifth Form at St. Dominic's" (Read half). "Nature and the Poet." Wordsworth. (Summarize.) "Twelfth Night." Continue 2nd Scene, ten lines. Select Prose Extract.
Show how far Britain is self-supporting and how far dependent in: Commodities, Trade.	Make a Clay Model of River Valley, Mtn. Range.	*Debate.* Children and Cinema Shows. *Essay.* Story of Ireland. *Telegram* enquiring for watch left behind at holiday boarding house. *Describe* the most striking advertisement you have seen. *Analyze* a poem.	"Fifth Form at St. Dominic's" (Read to end). "Realm of Fancy." Keats. Short notes and favourite lines. "Twelfth Night." Scene continued. Memorize Prose Extract.
In India and Canada, mention and describe all special regions of industry.	Make a Cardboard Model of C.P.R.	*Debate.* L.C.C. Economy. *Essay.* The "Quest." *Make a list* of chief points you would expect from a boy or girl seeking situation in your office. The Use of the Telephone. Three Nouns from Verbs. Three Verbs from Adjectives. Three Adjectives from Adverbs.	"Fifth Form at St. Dominic's" (Short argument of Story). "Ode to Autumn." Keats. (Paraphase any twelve lines.) "Twelfth Night." (Fully describe two characters.) Select Historical Poem.
Draw Sketch Map of, and describe, Asia Minor. Show its main communications.	Make a Cardboard Model of Globe, colouring Climatic Belts.	*Debate.* Domestic Centres. *Essay.* London Sales. *Make out* handbill for entertainment in aid of Local Charity. "Myself." A description. Give examples of: Direct and Indirect Speech. Active and Passive Voice. Direct and Indirect Object.	"Fifth Form at St. Dominic's." Characters, Scenes, } Notes. Setting. Make lists, with authors, of poems on Birds, Flowers, Seasons, Love. Memorize Historical Poem.

EN FINISHED ASSIGNMENT).

Subject;
l Subject (to aid future career), but
jects Studied.

ASSIGNMENTS

FROM ELEMENTARY SCHOOLS WORKING ON THE DALTON PLAN WITHOUT SPECIALIZATION

One teacher assigns the work to be done by her own class in all subjects. In this same way the Dalton Plan could be used by teachers of ungraded or rural schools.

A

See Contract Assignment Chart, folded insert

B

Corrections to be done first

ARITHMETIC. Longman, pp. 29 and 30.

ENGLISH. Lay, Exercises 30, 30. Write from *memory* "Winter."

Write your impressions of Westminster Abbey.

LITERATURE. Read two more "Parables from Nature" stories. Write titles in literature books of all the Parables and poems you know.

GEOGRAPHY. Lay's "Europe," chaps. 3 and 4.

Questions:

1. Draw a sketch map of the English Channel with the help of the book; then without the book, put in the chief ports (both French and English) and ocean routes.

2. Giving about five lines to each, tell what you know of the following: Landes, Seine and its basin, Paris, Riviera, and Marseilles.

3. What is the importance of: (*a*) Toulon, (*b*) Canal du Midi, (*c*) Lille?

   What are the most important products of France?

HISTORY. "The New Liberty," pp. 32–51.

Questions:

1. As concisely as possible give the character of Henry VIII.
2. What do you know of: (*a*) the Battle of the Spurs, (*b*) the Battle of Flodden Field?
   Give the causes, results, and dates in both cases.
3. Describe the character of Thomas Wolsey; give the chief events in his life.
4. Explain fully why Luther has been given such a high place in the world's history.

PAPER L

GEOGRAPHY. "Russia, MacKinder." 266–274.
Lay, 91–103.

Questions:

1. Prepare 103–104, Lay.
2. Sketch map on p. 98, Lay.

Reference Book: Herbertoors, 63–66.

ENGLISH.

1. Prepare a speech.
2. Write a letter to a miser pointing out the absurdity of his life. Be courteous and convincing.
3. Spelling. L. March 68–73.
4. Study "The Merchant of Venice."

HISTORY. Oliver Cromwell. John Drinkwater.
Piers Plowman. 92–101.

Questions:

1. Had you been alive in the Civil War on what side would you have been on and why?
2. Your opinion of Wentworth: what makes you hold that opinion?
3. State briefly what led to the Civil War.
4*a*. What do you know of the Ironsides?
4*b*. What was the Self Denying Ordnance? Why was it necessary.

APPENDIX II

ASSIGNMENTS WHICH HAVE BEEN USED IN THE COUNTY SECONDARY SCHOOL, STREATHAM

HISTORY SYLLABUS IX

FORM IV

AGED 14.

Subjects for Study:

The Commonwealth, 1649–1660.

1. The different attempts to rule England after death, 1649.
2. The Foreign Policy of Cromwell.
3. Failure of the Puritan Rule under Richard Cromwell. Events leading to the return of the King.

1. ATTEMPTS TO RULE ENGLAND.

1. Notice King and House of Lords abolished. A Council of State established. What really was the power behind this?
2. Study how Cromwell tried to rule with Parliament. Why did the rule of the Saints' (Barebone's) Parliament fail?
3. Army now plans Instrument of Government, 1653. Make notes on its terms. Notice how Cromwell still attempts to rule with Parlia-

ment. Failure—because that body refuses to
govern, but discusses instead.

4. Government now falls back to the Army. Note
the powers of the Major-Generals. Why were
they hated?

5. LAST OF CROMWELL'S PARLIAMENTS.
Study the document Humble Petition and
Advice. What addition was made to the Gov-
ernment?

Notice Cromwell's work in Scotland and Ireland
to crush the Royalists.

Exercise: How far did Cromwell carry out in his
government the principles for which Parliament
had fought in the Civil War?

2. CROMWELL'S FOREIGN POLICY.

1. Study the ideas underlying Cromwell's relations
with foreign countries. Note his attitude to
France, Spain, and Holland. Make an estimate of his prestige amongst foreign powers.

2. Notice the use of the Fleet in (1) capture of
Jamaica, 1655, (2) destruction of pirates, (3)
war with Holland.

3. EVENTS BETWEEN DEATH OF CROMWELL AND RESTORA-
TION OF CHARLES II, 1660.

(*a*) Study character of Richard Cromwell and his
failure to rule

(*b*) Notice carefully signs which indicate a desire
to return to old methods of government.

(*c*) Part played by the Army and General Monk.

(*d*) Declaration of Breda. Return of Charles II.
Where had he been? Terms of return.

Think over and discuss the following questions:
Was the Civil War in vain, as the Commonwealth
was overthrown on the return of the King? What

good to England remained as a legacy from the
period of Puritan rule?

Books: Warner and Marten, Part II; Tout; Thomson; "Piers Plowman," Book VII; "Documents," pp.
571–586; Milton's "Poems on Cromwell"; Novel:
"Woodstock," by Scott.

GEOGRAPHY SYLLABUS IX

For Girls of 15, after a year's work on the British Isles

LOWER V (4 periods per week)

Subject for Study:

**A survey of the commerce of the British Isles—the
reasons for the position of the United Kingdom in
the trade of the world.**

    1. NATURAL ADVANTAGES OF BRITISH ISLES.

        Study the position of British Isles with regard
        to Europe and the surrounding seas. World
        position. Note harbours, river mouths, and
        ports. Think over the advantages of the
        climate of British Isles and the consequences
        of these advantages upon products.

    2. OUR FOOD SUPPLY.

        Make a survey of *agriculture* during the last
        twenty years.

Home   Notice home supply of *meat* and its inade-
supplies.   quacy. Study the *fishing* industry, distribution of fish for home and export consumption.

Foreign   From where do we obtain wheat and other

Supplies.   grains? Source of our meat supplies, fruit and dairy produce from across sea.

3. THE INDUSTRIES OF BRITISH ISLES.

Study the *textile* industries.

Notice those with home supplies of raw material.

Notice those with foreign supplies of raw material.

Make a careful study of the "Associated Industries" (dyeing, bleaching, chemicals, soap-making, oil-refining).

Find out all you can of the *iron and steel industry*.

Chief centres of engineering and shipbuilding. Coal trade.

4. TRANSPORT.

Internal.—Railway versus road—the modern problem for passengers and goods.

Find out new air services to the Continent, and times taken.

5. EXPORT AND IMPORT TRADE.

Summarize this trade of the United Kingdom, noting the country and destination of export, and country of origin of import.

Exercises.—Answer one of the following:
1. Point out the relation of quick, cheap transport to trade. How does the transport problem affect Britain's external and internal trade?
2. Explain the dependence of the United Kingdom upon foreign supplies of raw material. How far is the British Empire self-supporting?

Books: Atlas (notice also maps on board); Chambers' "Commercial Geography"; Adams' "Commercial Geography"; Howarth's "Commercial Geography"; "Britain and British Seas," chap. i, ii, xiv, xv, xix; "Natural Wealth of Britain," chaps. xvii-xxii. Look up the "Times Trade Supplements"; Daily Newspapers.

ENGLISH

SUMMER TERM 1922

AGED 14   FORM IV   1ST MONTH

"Macbeth."

Read Acts I and II. Act I, 1: What purpose is served by this scene? Act I, 2: Give meaning of kerns, gallow-glass, Golgotha. Why does king confer title on Macbeth? Write a summary of happenings from Act II, beginning to end.
Learn Act I, 5, lines 13–28.

"Poems of Homeland," Book II.

Read "POEMS ON HOME," Section VI.
What impressions of British Isles would these poems give you if you were a foreigner?
Which poem do you think contains the most beautiful descriptions? Quote and give your impressions.
Which shows deepest patriotic feeling?
Does any poem strike you as being rather false in sentiment? If so, why?

"LONDON RIVER."
Why is poem written in this metre?
Write out simply what the poem is about.

Write out phrases which strongly suggest sound;
phrases which sound fine or beautiful.

What passage seems most to suggest the flow of the
river?

What characteristics of the English does this poem
speak of?

Give one example of following: alliteration, antithesis, onomatopoeia.

Grammar.

Read HARRISON, chap. xiv, p. 102, then do ⎫ Analysis
Ex. III, p. 104.   ⎬ of
Read HARRISON, chap. xv, p. 104, then do ⎭ Complex
Ex. I, p. 106.   Sentences.

Make a table of Pronouns: Personal, Relative, Interrogative, Demonstrative, Possessive.

Make a table of Adjectives: Interrogative, Demonstrative, Possessive.

Composition.

1. Write a letter of sympathy to a dear friend who
has just suffered some grave hardship.
2. Write 20 lines in the metre of "Lay of Last
Minstrel," describing Streatham or Tooting
Common. Begin:
"The common stretches broad and green."
3. Write an original story called "The Ghost of Willow Glen."

Middle. Learn any other 20 lines from "Macbeth."

Higher. Read Shakespeare's life in "Cyclopaedia of
Literature."

LATIN SYLLABUS

2ND YEAR

AGE 15   LOWER V   7TH MONTH

1ST WEEK

Syntax.

Learn DAKERS' "JUNIOR LATIN PROSE," §§ 61–66.
This covers the construction of Questions, Direct
and Indirect.

Read §§ 18, 21, noting carefully the examples of
Latin adjectives used for English adverbs.

Prose.

Write in Latin, Extracts 118 and 122, NORTH AND
HILLARD'S "LATIN PROSE COMPOSITION."

Note that these contain many examples of Indirect
Questions. Try sometimes to use the Ablative
Absolute and subordinate clauses instead of prin-
cipal clauses.

Vocabulary.

Learn perfectly Vocabularies 64–69, and think of
some picture for the description of which you might
use these words.

OVID, Extracts I–IV. Before you begin this there will
be a lesson on metre.

CAESAR, Book iv, chap. xx, xxi.

For Higher Division.

Describe how the Romans would attack a fortified
place. See picture cards, and Livingstone and
Freeman, Introduction.

Learn Latin terms.

N.B. Poetry (Ovid) is to be the most important part of our **Translation** this term, but we cannot afford to neglect prose translation (Caesar) altogether, both for its own sake, and also because it will help us in our prose.

2ND WEEK

Syntax.

Dependent Clauses in "ORATIO OBLIQUA." DAKERS, §§ 58, 59.
Study, as a revision, the examples in §§ 22–24; 31–34; 37–41.

Prose.

NORTH AND HILLARD, Extract 125, for practice in Syntax studied in (a), and Extract 136 which will test your back work. You will find notes and suggestions on the board.

Vocabulary.

70–75. 75 is very important. Picture different people as the subjects of the verbs.

Translation.

OVID, Extracts V and VI.

CAESAR, iv, 22 and 23.

Higher Division.
Draw a picture of a Roman camp, describe it, and learn the Latin terms.

Syntax.

The Relative with the Subjunctive. DAKERS, § 57.
Revision (thorough) of Final and Consecutive
Clauses, §§ 47–50; 52–55.

Prose.

Write Extract 158, NORTH AND HILLARD. Revise your
notes on verbs of *Fearing*.
Write Exercise 146 for practice of the Relative with
Subjunctive. You should manage without notes,
but if you are in difficulties, you may consult notes
on board.

Vocabulary.

76–79. Make a short story (English), bringing in as
many of these words as possible. This will help
you to remember.

Translation.

OVID, Extracts VII and VIII to line 20.
CAESAR, iv, 24, 25.

Higher Division.

Describe the Roman artillery (Ballistae, Catapultae,
Scorpiones).
   (*a*) Study pictures.
   (*b*) Study picture of a Roman soldier. Describe
       his clothing, his armour, and his weapons.

4TH WEEK

Syntax.

Causal Sentences. DAKERS, §§ 67, 68. Revision of the Supines. See notes and DAKERS, §§ 111, 112. Revise notes on translation of *must*.

Prose.

NORTH AND HILLARD, Exercises 150–152.
Translate only the expressions containing *must* in these three exercises.
Extract 162. See notes on board.

Vocabulary.

80–84. Many of these words you know. Devote your attention to *new* ones, especially to 84.

Translation.

OVID. Finish Extract VIII and IX.
CAESAR, iv, 26, 27.

Higher Divisions.

How many men in a legion? What were the divisions of a legion? Who were the officers? What can you find out about a soldier's (*a*) pay; (*b*) food.

GEOMETRY. *Syllabus I*

Form II. Age 11

3rd Week. Jan. 28th

Here are two revision problems. Can you do them?
1. A man notices that angle of elevation of top of a tower is 30°; on walking 300 ft. nearer it is 60°. What is its height?
2. A man standing at a point o takes the following bearings: church 47°, castle 115°, mountain 190°, hayrick 245°, flagstaff 280°, inn 320°. Draw diagram and show direction of these places.

Here are some interesting problems in mensuration. Draw simple plans where necessary; work clearly and neatly.
1. A garden consists of a lawn with a path round it. The garden is 55 ft. long and 40 ft. broad, and the path 5 ft. wide. Find area of the path.
2. An oblong garden is 135 ft. by 50 ft.; it has paths 3 ft. wide running the whole length of its two long sides. Find area of paths and grass.
3. If the area of a garden is 300 sq. ft., and its breadth 15 ft., what is its length?
4. Find area of (*a*) top of examination desk; (*b*) top of small collapsible table; (*c*) top of large table.

The above examples must be done by *everyone*. Only *quick* girls may attempt the

Middle Syllabus

1. What is the difference between a square foot and one foot square?
2. How many ¾-in. squares of glass will fill a rectangle 18 in. by 10½ in.?

3. Out of a piece of paper 7¾ in. square, a rectangle
4½ in. by 3½ in. is cut. How many sq. in left?
If you are *very* quick you may try the

Higher Syllabus

1. Wall paper is sold in rolls, 12 yds. long by 21 in.
wide. What is area of a roll? How many rolls
are needed for a room 17½ ft. by 13½ ft. by
12¹/₂ ft. high, allowing 17²/₃ sq. yds. for windows,
etc., and supposing ⅛ of paper is wasted?
2. What would it cost to varnish a border, 2 ft. wide,
round a room 15 ft. long by 22 ft. broad, at 1¼d.
per sq. ft.?

MATHEMATICS

Form Lower V. Age 15

* Hall and Stevens, "School Geometry" (Macmillan
and Co.), Chignell and Paterson (Oxford
Press), Part II.

1st Week

Revise Theorems 32, 34, 35, 38, 39, 40, 41. Theorems on
chord properties and angle properties of a circle.
Lower. P. 147, nos. 1–6; p. 149, 8–12; p. 151, 1 and 2.
" 153, " 1–4; " 163, 1 and 2; p. 165, 1–6.

[Typical examples (p. 147, 5): Describe a circle that shall
pass through two given points and have its centre on a given
straight line. When is this impossible?
P. 165, 5: A straight rod of given length slides between
two straight rulers placed at right angles to one another;
find the locus of its middle point.]

Middle. P. 151, no. 3.　　　　P. 163, 3 and 4.
Higher. " 151, nos. 4 and 5　　" 163, 5.

* The examples are included here by kind permission of the
publishers.

2ND WEEK

1. Find the area of a triangle whose sides are
   (a) 7.34 in., 4.62 in., 5.49 in. [Use Pythagoras.]
   (b) Find the area of the same triangle by using
       the formula,

$$A = \sqrt{s(s-a)(s-b)(s-c)} \text{ where } A = \text{area.}$$
$$S = \tfrac{1}{2} \text{ perimeter.}$$

   a, b, c, are the sides opposite the angles, A, B. C.
2. Two cubes whose edges are 3.46 in. and 5.72 in.
   are melted and recast in the shape of a cube.
   Find the length of its edge.
   Revise Theorems 42-49. Theorems on arcs and
   angles in a circle, Tangency, Contact of Circles,
   Alternate Segment.

Lower. P. 170, nos. 1, 2, 3, 13–21.   P. 177, nos. 1–15.
     " 179, " 1–10   " 181, " 1–3.
Middle. " 170, " 11, 12   " 181, " 4–6.
Higher. " 170, " 6–10, 19, 20, 22 " 181 completed.

[Typical examples (p. 170, no. 3): Two circles intersect
at A and B; and through A any straight line P A Q is drawn
terminated by the circumferences. Show that P Q subtends
a constant angle at B.
   P. 179, no. 6: A straight line is drawn through the point
of contact of two circles whose centres are A and B, cutting
the circumferences at P and Q respectively. Show that the
radii AP and BQ are parallel.]

3RD WEEK

1. An isosceles △ has its equal sides 4.62 in. long
   and a base of 2.84 in. Find the area. Find
   also the length of the perpendicular from either
   extremity of the base to the opposite side.

2. Find the volume of a cylinder whose diameter is 4.234 in., and whose height is 28.32 in. Find also the area of its curved surface.

Problems 21–29: Circles, Common Tangents, Construction of triangles given different elements, triangles, and circles.

Lower. P. 187, nos. 1–7; p. 189, nos. 1–11; p. 191, 1, 2, 3. " 198 " 1–4 " 199 " 1–12.

Middle. " 187 " 8 " 191 " 4 " 198, 5.

Higher. " 187 " 9 " 191 " 5, 6, 7.

[Typical examples (p. 187, no. 5): Draw two circles with radii 1.6 in. and 0.8 in., and with their centres 3.0 in. apart. Draw all their common tangents.

P. 191, no. 2. Construct a triangle having given the base, the vertical angle, and

1. One other side; 2. The altitude; 3. The length of the median which bisects the base; 4. The foot of the perpendicular from the vertex to the base.]

4TH WEEK

1. A triangle has an area of 47.6 sq. cm., and one side is 8.4 cm. What is the length of the perpendicular to that side from the opposite vertex?

2. (*a*) Obtain a formula for the area of a regular hexagon of side "*a.*"
   (*b*) Calculate the area of a regular hexagon of side 4.3 in.

3. A hollow sphere of external diameter 10 in. and made of metal 1 in. thick, is melted down and recast as a solid sphere. Find the diameter of the solid sphere.

Problems 30, 31, in- and escribed regular polygons. Pp. 207, 208—pedal triangle orthocentre.

Lower. P. 200, nos. 2, 3, 4; p. 205, nos. 1–12; p. 201, 1, 2, 3; p. 206, nos. 1–4, 11; p. 209, nos. 1–3.

Middle. P. 201, nos. 4; p. 206, nos. 5, 6, 7, 9; p. 209, 4–7.

Higher. P. 206, nos. 8–12; p. 209, nos. 8–12.

[Typical examples (p. 205, 8): Find to the nearest tenth of an inch the side of a square whose area is equal to that of a circle of radius 5 in.

P. 206, 7: In any triangle the difference of two sides is equal to the difference of the segments into which the third side is divided at the point of contact of the inscribed circle.]

ENGLISH SYLLABUS

FORM 1A.   AGE 10

WEEK ENDING JAN. 14TH

Poetry. FRIDAY.

Copy into own Poetry Book four verses of Thomas the Rymer, and if time do an illustration. Learn the four verses (any other poem of your own choice may be learnt as well).

Literature. ADVENTURES OF ODYSSEUS, chap. xiv.

Write this for Thursday in Reading Book.

1. Imagine you are Odysseus; then write out a short account of the way the swineherd welcomed you at Ithaca. Explain why he would not believe what you said.

N.B. You will find it easier to do if you imagine you are telling someone—Telemachus, for example—all about the adventure.

2. Write down any words difficult to spell in own English Book.

Composition. MONDAY.

1. Refer again to GREENWOOD TREE, p. 198, and if you don't remember the story read again "The Man in the Moon."

2. Write a scene between the Old Man and the Stranger, and any other people. Do not use only the words in the book, but try to imagine what they might have said to one another.

N.B. Remember to write at the beginning the characters you introduce, and the place where the scene takes place.

Extra English.

Go on reading HINDU TALES, and write the answers to each chapter as you go along.
[Do all the other English first.]

PROGRAMME DU FRANÇAIS

CLASSE IVA

1ᴱᴿ TRIMESTRE   3ᴱ MOIS   AGE 14

Lecture pour le Mois: "Remi en Angleterre," chap. iii, Père et mère honoreras.

1ᴿᴱ SEMAINE

A savoir le vocabulaire de chap. xxi, ALLPRESS (p. 42), et l'exercice sur la formation des mots (p. 4).

2ᴱ SEMAINE

GRAMMAIRE: Règles du subjonctif, p. 112, § 117, § 119, § 120. à savoir par cœur les listes.
VOCABULAIRE: voir feuille spéciale (Remi).
VERBES: conclure, moudre, coudre.
DICTÉE: arrangée sur la grammaire et le vocabulaire appris.

EXERCICE (en classe). Allpress, Ex. 21, p. 160.   III et IV.

(écrit). *Lower:* 5 phrases. *Middle:* 7 phrases choisies dans IV (1–15). *Upper:* première partie de IV, 16.

3ᴹᴱ SEMAINE

GRAMMAIRE: à revoir les règles du subjonctif.

VERBES: se souvenir, se plaire, se taire.

A APPRENDRE PAR CŒUR: "L'histoire de Louis XIV et du comédien."

VOCABULAIRE: feuille spéciale.

LECTURE FACULTATIVE: 20 pages d'un des LIVRES ROSES. (To be tested by Mistress.)

EXERCICE FACULTATIF: une lettre en français de Remi à la mère Barberin, lui disant comment il a trouvé ses parents.

Take note.

1. During the first week of the month there will be a lesson each day. This leaves only forty minutes' work to be done in your free time either at home or at school.

2. You will notice that the chapter from "Remi en Angleterre" set for reading during the month has not been divided up. Divide it up as you please. Save your difficulties for a group lesson, the third period on Friday, March 17th.

3. A *special star* may be obtained for
   (*a*) Specially good conversational work.
   OR (*b*) The LECTURE FACULTATIVE (see front page).
   (*c*) The EXERCICE FACULTATIF (see front page).

PROGRAMME DU FRANÇAIS

Upper V Remove (Matriculation Form)

Trimestre, Moise. Classe de Age

1ᵉ Semaine

Degré inférieur.
    Lire. Bowen. French Lyrical Poetry.
      (*a*) Le Chant du Départ.
      (*b*) Couplets militaires.
      (*c*) Ronde patriotique.
    Ecrire. Vocabulaire inconnu au carnet.
    Apprendre. Vocabulaire.

Moyen.
Ce qui précède et:

    Préparer. Minssen, "Composition," les nos. 144, 145.
    Apprendre. Bowen, "Extase."
    Ecrire en Français. Minssen, 147.
    Ecrire en Anglais. Bowen, "Le coin du feu."

Supérieur.

    Petite narration, précédée d'un plan.
    Sujet: Un orage au mois d'avril.
    N.B. Toute élève devra écrire la narration.

2ᵉ Semaine

Degré inférieur.

    Lire. Daudet, "La Mule du Pape."
    Apprendre. Daudet, "De tous . . . huit jours."
    Ecrire. Vocabulaire inconnu.

Moyen.

Ce qui précède et:

PRÉPARER. Oran. Nos. 2, 16, 19.
ECRIRE. Oran. Nos. 5, 18.
ECRIRE EN FRANCAIS. Résumé de "La petite Fodette."
ECRIRE EN ANGLAIS. Daudet (p. 71), "Quand . . .
   Camangue."

Supérieur.

Petite narration, précédée d'un plan.
Sujet: un orage au mois d'avril.
   N.B. Toute élève devra écrire la narration. Résumé
   que ce soit des phrases courtes, dont chacune
   fera étape.

PROGRAMME DU FRANÇAIS

UPPER V REMOVE (MATRICULATION FORM)

TRIMESTRE, MOIS. CLASSE DE AGE 17

1ᴱ SEMAINE

Theme. { *Upper.* Duhamel, 94. *The Cat's Pilgrimage.*
{ *Lower.* Duhamel et Minssen, 132. *The Chair*
{   *stuffer's donkey.*
Literature. Alfred de Musset—l'homme.
Lecture. Hernani. On ne badine pas avec l'amour.
Notre Dame de Paris. Poèmes lydiques.
   Corriger les fautes faites à l'examen.

2ᴱ SEMAINE

Theme. Les mêmes—suite (Duhamel, 95. D. and
Minssen, 133).

Literature. Alfred de Musset—le poète des nuits.
Lecture. Les mêmes—suite. Aussi *les Nuits.*
Essai. *La Nuit de Décembre.*

3ᴱ Semaine

Theme. {
Upper. Même—suite Duhamel, 96.
Lower. Duhamel et Minssen, 4. *Murder of Marshal d'Ancre.*
}

Literature. Molière.
Lecture. Les mêmes—suite.
Essai. On ne badine pas avec l'amour (compte rendu) *ou* Compte rendu 1ᵉʳ chapitre de *Notre Dame de Paris.*

4ᴱ Semaine

Theme. {
Upper. The Cat's Pilgrimage. Suite et fin. Duhamel, 97.
Lower. Murder of Marshal d'Ancre. Suite et fin. D. and M., 5.
}

Literature. Hernani.
Lecture. Les mêmes—suite et fin, excepté *Notre Dame de Paris.*
Essai. Préparer un compte rendu de *Hernani.*

SOME OPINIONS OF BRITISH ELEMEN-TARY HEAD MISTRESSES AND CHIL-DREN ON THE DALTON PLAN

OPINIONS OF HEAD MISTRESSES IN ELEMEN-TARY SCHOOLS WHERE THE DALTON PLAN HAS BEEN PUT INTO OPERATION.

LONDON, S.E.

"In the four upper classes of the Girls' Section, where the children range in age from nine to fourteen, we have been working on the Dalton Laboratory Plan for the past six months; and in the lower classes, some of the more intelligent children, aged from seven to nine, have also been drawn into it for special subjects. Though our school is designed for 250 pupils we have at present 277, so that each class numbers from forty to forty-five children. Our class-rooms have been converted into laboratories, but lack of space necessitates two subjects to each room. As, however, we study major subjects in the morning and minor subjects in the afternoon, we do not find this arrangement inconvenient. Thus Mathematics shares a laboratory with Handicrafts and the English laboratory is also used for Hygiene, each class-teacher taking the two subjects and in some cases a third subject as well. We overcome the difficulty created by the widely varying powers and speed of individual children belonging to the same class by dividing the assignments into maximum, medium, and minimum. In this way the quick and clever children are not kept back by the slow ones.

"At the beginning of our experiment we certainly had some difficulty in getting the children to settle down to work and to assume responsibility in measuring their own time. But as they became accustomed to their new liberty the confusion of the first days subsided. All our teachers are unanimous in declaring that more work and better work has been done under the Dalton method than under the old system. Even the dearth of sufficient books to go round seems to have bred a spirit of helpfulness among the pupils. We use the graph to record progress, and on the back of the card a conduct graph has been added with the letters of the alphabet to indicate lapses from our standard of discipline—A $= 1$ lapse, $B = 2$ lapse, and so on.

"From the teacher's point of view we do find the Dalton Plan entails much heavier work. At first I found class-mistresses spending half their nights in composing assignments and correcting work, and I seriously feared we might have to abandon the new method on that account. None of them were, however, willing to do so and we have now to some extent got over this difficulty by reducing the amount of work required in the assignments. Personally I think it essential not to set too high a standard of work especially at the beginning. If any of the children finishes her assignment before the end of the week or month, I have found a few hours or even a day of quiet reading an excellent way of filling up the time. Of course every child is free to choose her book and they seem to enjoy this extra opportunity of studying a weak subject. Here specialization appeals to our teachers, as providing them with a chance of increasing their knowledge, and some of them regret that the system does not permit them to devote all their energy to one subject."

London, W.

"Here so far we have only reorganized one class in the Girls' Section on the Dalton Laboratory Plan. But the results of our six months' trial have proved so satisfactory that we hope to extend it to two more classes next term. We would not go back to the former method for anything. The effect on the children is marvellous. Not only do they take a real pleasure in their work now but under the Dalton Plan they accomplish far more than before. We also find the children more sympathetic towards each other. As there are between thirty and forty pupils in this particular class, each group engaged in the same subject chooses a helper from among its members to whom those in difficulties can go when the reader is taken up with another child or another subject. These helpers are the older and more intelligent girls, and the class-mistress is of course always there to check the help they give and to supplement it. In addition to this she has started a log-book in which all the pupils' names are entered. Against them she writes her criticisms of the work of each one after she has gone over it, adding a word of advice on general progress. This book is always available for any pupil to refer to. These devices have enabled the teacher to cope with the far greater demands which the Dalton Plan makes on her time and knowledge. They also enable the pupil to find immediate assistance in solving any difficulties that may arise when she is left to her own resources. My teachers show no inclination to limit their work to teaching only one subject in the curriculum. They seem to think such specialization narrowing to the mental outlook. As the bulk of children in Elementary Schools finish their education at fourteen, the average teacher should surely be able to meet the demand in all standard subjects."

OPINIONS OF BRITISH ELEMENTARY SCHOOL CHILDREN ON THE DALTON PLAN

CLASS I   6.12.21

1. I do like the plan by which we are working. (*a*) I like to find the information from books, (*b*) and to change a subject when I feel tired of it. (*c*) When I feel I would like to study, I can do so, but before, on the old system, I could not have done so. (*d*) On this plan we have the afternoons clear for the other subjects, so I like this plan very much.

2. I did not like the plan when we first began, I could not get into it, it seemed peculiar. I understood the scheme, but I could not work by it at first. But I like it now. I do not know what the exact trouble was, only that I could not seem to work by it.

3. I cannot find any faults about the Dalton Plan, only, perhaps (*a*) when I am interested in the study it is time to go home for dinner, perhaps that is called a fault, or even, I do not very much like (*b*) copying the assignment down on Friday afternoons, but these faults are very slight, (*c*) and I should like some more oral lessons.

4. There are not sufficient books for the girls to have; for example, there are only two "Piers Plowman," VI, and most of the girls want them at once. So it would be very nice to have some more books for next term.

CLASS I

1. I like the plan because formerly I was content with a surface knowledge, letting the teachers give me all the good they had got out of a book, and getting everything they had thought out without first thinking it

out myself, so that I grew to rely on them more and more, and had hardly an idea for myself on any subject. Now, I look through perhaps two or three books, and when I find something really good, I feel as though I had made a new discovery, and thus it makes me much keener and more interested. Besides, when we are given our week's assignment, there are always some new problems which are fascinating to work out, and when I think I have solved the problem it gives me fresh interest, because I feel as if I were getting on much better. We have to rely on our own effort now, so that we are always on the look-out for something fresh on our subjects, and take a universal (I mean as far universal as we can get) interest in the things going on around us; and whereas we looked for interest in, say, only one subject, we now have interest in them all.

Also the plan gives us more time to concentrate on the different subjects, though this is where I think that the plan is not so good, because though we are given about the same time for working as before, we are required to read a great many more books, and write a great many more exercises. I don't think anybody gets her work done in school hours, unless it is very much the minimum. But, of course, we don't grudge the time one little bit, only if we had more time we could spare more time on the extra work.

It also teaches us our weaknesses very much more than if we just learnt the lessons in which we are weak, without finding the causes and effects, and so on. It is just like having to forage for one's food; you learn more of the animals and Nature than if we spent a twelvemonth trying to learn their ways in an academy or university, while living on the food which is received and manufactured by others.

2. I think that the suddenness of the plan took away our breaths. Besides, I did not wish to change the old plan, under which we had worked so long, for a new

one whose very ideas were new. The teachers, our old supports, would be gone, and the harder work was not very welcome, especially when we had got fairly comfortable in the old groove. We did not fit our subjects to the time either, and found when the week was up, we had scarcely begun one subject, or hardly finished another.

CLASS II 7.12.21

1. I think it is a very good plan and I like it much better than the old plan. It gives us more time to get on and we do not have to wait for others. We can get on all right ourselves, but it gives the teachers more working.

2. I think the trouble is that we did not quite know how to get on alone, and we were not used to it, and I think some of us were impatient about the books.

3. We sometimes have to wait for books, which cannot be helped.

4. I think we could have twenty minutes' play in the afternoons instead of ten minutes in the morning.

5. We could each bring some small sum of money to help buy new books.

6. As the four top classes are using this Dalton Plan I think we could have a room for each subject.

CLASS II 7.12.21

1. I think the Dalton Plan is much better and much more interesting because we are much more free and can find out things for ourselves, whereas before we only knew what was told us by teachers.

2. At the beginning of the term we were used to being told everything and were not at all familiar with our books. We did not know in which book to look for the best descriptions of any point, or to find out what our books really contained.

3. Although I appreciate the plan I think that it has several drawbacks: (i) When only one book has a point which all the class has to study, some girls are unable to do their work. (ii) There is more moving about.

CLASS II 7.12.21

1. I do like the new way and plan of working in which I am able to study more by myself. It has many good points, for example, one need not stop in the middle of a lesson to continue with a different kind of subject.

2. When we first started this new Dalton Plan it was such a change from the old plan that we could not really settle to our work and therefore some of us did not get our week's assignment finished.

3. There are a few faults: (*a*) There is only one book to go round the whole class, and that is a drawback because sometimes a girl does not get the book. (*b*) The Geography and History room is crowded and some girls have to go into their own class room and most likely change their subjects. At first the break at 10 o'clock was very inconvenient to the teachers, but as it is altered it is much better and wiser.

4. We need more books to go round the class. This plan is very wise, but it would be wiser if we could work in the afternoons by this new plan, and also in Science, Hygiene, and a few games. If we could start earlier, we should have more time for play.

Aged 5/12 years CLASS III 6.12.21

1. I like the Dalton plan very much, it is an interesting way of working. In the History and Geography we get on at our own pace and can learn more by the plan, whereas before, when we had separate lessons the sharp girls had to wait for the slow ones. It is the same with the arithmetic, the girls who could get on

and get the sums done had to wait for the others, but now we can do them any time during the two hours we are given. In the time, just before the exams, much more revision can be done which helps us to take higher places in the exams. It also teaches us to help ourselves and not always have the teacher watching over us.

2. At the beginning of the term, when we first started the plan, I did not like it very much. It was new and we weren't used to working that way, but when we settled down it was quite alright and I think most of us like it now.

Aged 11, 5/12 years   CLASS III   6.12.21

1. I like the Dalton plan very much; and I think it very much better because if we could not get on with one subject, or could not set our mind on it, we could do another subject, and then come back to it again. Again, if we had not quite finished a subject at an appointed time, we could spend a few minutes longer at it, whereas if we were not using this plan, we would have to stop, and the work would be unfinished. I think, too, by being able to finish our work we can learn more; or if one week we had a subject which was very easy, and got it done quickly, we could spend more time at another.

2. At the beginning of the term we thought we would never get the work finished, and so hurried through it and consequently never grasped the work we were supposed to learn; but in two or three weeks' time, when we began to grasp the plan, we found that if we worked carefully we could get it all done.

3. I have no fault to find in the plan I simply think it's ripping.

Aged 12 years CLASS III 6.12.21

1. The idea of the new plan is very pleasing to me. For instance, when I am just getting wrapt up in some study and the half hour is gone, I can go on until I have finished the chapter. We are free.

2. My trouble at the beginning of the term was this: (*a*) I thought I should not be finished my work at the end of the week. (*b*) We were left to ourselves, whereas before, our teacher took us with our lessons. (*c*) I was not quite used to it.

3. The faults of the plan are not many, to my idea. One is, that there is so much walking about to be done. Another is, catching up to other girls if you are away. A third fault is, that Miss Gibbs's books which she lends to us to help us in History and Geography may get frightfully spoilt in time.

Aged 12 years CLASS III 6.12.21

1. I appreciate the plan very much. I feel more interested while doing the work by myself, and the quick and intelligent girls need not wait for the slow ones, but learn more and more to get ahead of them.

2. Not a bit did I like this plan at the beginning of the term, as I could not understand it, and I thought I would not progress at all. This would also make me feel as if I did not want to work if I did not understand it, but as I was told more about it, I began to understand, and when the first morning of the new plan came I was feeling very glad.

3. The great fault I find that we do not have enough time to do our work in the morning, for sometimes when it is time to leave we are in the midst of a study. I sometimes do not like having to copy our contracts every Friday, for sometimes we have quite a lot.

4. I cannot suggest anything for the next term.

Aged 12 years   CLASS III   6.12.21

1. I do like this new plan of work, because I always seem to be able to get on quicker when working by myself. I also think that I can work much harder. The work seems easier now than it did before, for I do not like to have a teacher standing in front of me telling me what to do, I like to work by myself. This new plan seems to make me work harder, for I know that the work must be done, or else I shall be behind all the other girls, and I should not like that, so I do like this plan very much, and I hope that we always have to work by it.

2. I did not like the work at the beginning of the term, because it seemed so strange, and everything seemed to go wrong, and I could not get on with my work at all. I did not like going into the Geography and History room. I only went in there a few times but now I like going in there, and I have grown to like this plan very much indeed.

3. I cannot find any faults of the plan and I should not think that anybody could find any.

4. I cannot make any suggestions to help with the work next term, because I want to still keep going on with this same plan, and I want nothing to be altered in the least little bit, if it does I shall not like it, but I should like a few more holidays.

THE END.